The Seven Campfires of the Sioux

The Sacred Wisdom of the Lakota

The Seven Campfires of the Sioux

The Sacred Wisdom of the Lakota

Richard F. Epstein

****

The Seven Campfires of the Sioux: The Sacred Wisdom of the Lakota
Edition 2015
ISBN 13: 978-1517415433

****

Printed in the USA

TABLE OF CONTENTS

Preface

RAMAKRSIHNA

Romain Rolland called him the greatest teacher of modern times, and he said of him, "Allowing for the differences of country and time, Ramakrishna is the younger brother of Christ." It is said that two prominent avatars of the Hindu faith – Rama and Krishna – were incarnated into the body of this simple, ordinary man, who came to the world in the nineteenth century not to establish a new religion, but to revive a dying one, and to empower all religions and, indeed, all of humanity by his living example, proving that the similarities between the world community of religions are greater than the differences. He preached the eternal truths comprehensible to all, which would reach the innermost hearts of every man and woman. It is called Vedanta, a modern branch of the Vedas and Upanishads.

According to Swami Vivekananda, "Vedanta means the

end of the Vedas, the third section or Upanishads, containing the ripened ideas which we find more as gems in the earlier portion."1. The Vedanta teaches that man's real nature is divine, a manifestation of the infinite, immortal reality or Godhead which is within each person and every creature and object. The aim of a man or woman's life is to realize this divinity.

Christopher Isherwood in his book, Ramakrishna and His Disciples, called him a phenomenon. "This is the story of a phenomenon. I will begin by calling him simply that, rather than 'holy man,' 'mystic', 'saint', or 'avatar'; all emotive words with mixed association which may attract some readers, repel others. A phenomenon is something extraordinary and mysterious; most of all to those who were best fitted to understand him. A phenomenon is always a fact, an object of experience. That is how I shall try to approach Ramakrishna.2.

"In nineteenth century India, Ramakrishna revivified a tradition that was sinking under the dual burden of lifeless Hindu piety and the onslaught of English-imported Westernization. It was not a happy time for India. Neither was it a happy time for the West. Science and religion were at daggers drawn: a truce let alone common understanding seemed inconceivable. Rapid industrialization made human life seem cheap; the once cherished bonds that held people and society together were irretrievably frayed. During this time the East/West barrier became porous – a difficult adjustment for both parties. This best of times, worst of times scenario ushered in modernity with all its glory and confusion."3.

Ramakrishna came from the humblest beginnings, born to remarkably virtuous parents in the village of Kamarpukur on February 18, 1836.

During the early eighteen-fifties as a teenager, Ramakrishna arrived in Calcutta to live with his eldest brother. When his brother accepted the job of head priest in the temple of Dakshineswar, Ramakrishna accompanied him there. A short while later Ramakrishna became the chief priest of the Kali temple at Dakshineswar where he spent the duration of his life of 50 years.

For a period of sixteen years, from 1870 to the last day of his life, Ramakrishna practiced austere spiritual disciplines – not out of a need for perfection – because he was that already, but for the welfare of others.

Even though Ramakrishna was an avatar, almost from his inception on earth, like an ordinary human being, he had to struggle unceasingly for the vision he sought of his Ishtadeva or chosen ideal of God, which was the Divine Mother. Uppermost in his mind was the piercing idea of realizing God.

Since he dwelled under the yoke of maya (the illusion of substituting the real for the unreal) and existed in a human body even he was unsure. But there came a time when the ideal of seeing God took root in his mind and it became a powerful obsession. The consequences were serious. Ramakrishna became incapacitated. He could not laugh or perform even the simplest tasks. Comments Swami Vivekananda, "Often he would forget to place the food-offering before the image, sometimes he would forget to wave the light, at other times he would wave it for hours, and forget everything else."4. What was missing in his heart and soul was the vision of the Mother, and the intensity was so great that he could not continue to live without it.

Again Vivekananda, "And that one idea was in his mind every day: 'Is it true that Thou existest, O'Mother? Why dost Thou not speak? Art Thou dead?...Is there no one in this universe who can show the light unto me? Why send so many Messengers and not Thyself. Come to me? In this world of fights and factions whom am I to follow and believe? If Thou art the God of every man and woman alike why comest Thou not to speak to Thy Child and see if he is not ready.'"5.

Like yogis of every religion in the throes of austerities, the poor youth could only hang on, persisting to the end. Eventually, he lost all thought of himself, even neglecting to eat. A relative put food into his mouth, which he mechanically swallowed. "Days and nights thus passed with the boy. When a whole day would pass towards the evening when the peal of bells in the temples, and the voices singing would reach the wood where he stayed, it would make the boy very sad, and he would cry, 'Another day of this short life has gone and I have not known the truth.'"6.

"Years passed," writes Sister Nivedita, a prominent Western disciple of Vivekananda, "driven on by his own nature, impelled from within by that irresistible necessity that had called him into being, without one rest or relaxation, for twelve long years at least, he persisted in that inner warfare. Then, at last, the goal was attained. The Mother revealed Herself. From that moment his personality was that of a little child satisfied that he was in Her arms."7.

In the interim between the paramahamsa's (knower of Brahman) deep anguish of being separated from his chosen ideal, the Mother didn't leave him in the lurch completely, but her presence opened up to him gradually. Swami Vivekananda explains that, "The boy began to see visions, to see wonderful things, the secrets of his nature were beginning to open to him. Veil after veil was, as it were, being taken off. Mother, Herself, became the teacher and initialed the boy into the truths he sought."8.

But in his deep frustration in not fully realizing the Mother, Ramakrishna puts his vision into words. "[I felt] as if someone had taken hold of my heart and mind, and was wringing them like a wet towel. My eyes fell on the sword on the wall of the Mother's temple. I made up my mind to end my life that very moment. Like one mad I ran and caught hold of it, when suddenly I had the wonderful vision of the Mother and fell down unconscious. I did not know what happened then in the external world – how that day and the next slipped away. But in my heart of hearts there was flowing a current of intense bliss, never experienced before, and I had the immediate knowledge of the light that was the Mother. It was as if houses, doors, temples, and everything else vanished from my sight, leaving no trace whatever. However far and in whatever direction I looked I saw a continuous succession of effulgent waves rushing at me from all sides, with great speed. I was caught on the rush, and panting for breath I collapsed unconscious."9.

Was Ramakrishna's experience a charade? In a sense, he, as an incarnation forgot his true divine nature so he could be an exemplary for his disciples still on the path. Yet, like a method actor, he was aware of his own identity all throughout while he became the character he was portraying. Observes Vivekananda, "These Incarnations are conscious of their own divinity; they know it from their birth. They are like actors whose play is over, but who, after their work is done return to please others. These great ones are untouched by aught of earth; they assume our form and limitations for a time in order to teach us; but in reality they are never limited, they are ever free."10.

Ramakrishna, having realized the personification of his chosen ideal, the Divine Mother, could not sit still for this alone. He pursued other paths to God-realization espoused by other religions. He first pursued the dualistic and non-dualistic aspects of Hinduism and was quickly rewarded with the highest realization. Next he took up Islam. Thwarting Hindu custom and bias, he put on clothes in the Muslim fashion and requested Muslim cooking. Comments Pravrajika Vrajaprana, a Vedanta nun in California, "But Ramakrishna did it naturally and sincerely. He didn't do it to promote a cause or to satisfy some vague curiosity. God was so much the source of his life that he was compelled to experience him in every way possible. 'Cake tastes nice,' he would say, 'whichever way you eat it.'"11.

Next he took up Christianity, leaving behind temporarily Hindu attitudes and practices and became completely immersed in Christian sadhana (Spiritual practices, austerities), and to the amazement of his intimate inner circle of disciples, within a very short period, he experienced the mystical union with Christ.

Thus, one of the major cornerstones of Ramakrishna's message was to synthesize and harmonize the salient truths of all beliefs which he compared to sugar. Said the Paramahamsa, "We need to take out the sugar and leave the sand behind: we should extract the essence of religion – whether we call it union with God or Self-realization – and leave the rest behind. Whatever helps us to manifest our divinity we embrace; whatever pulls us away from that ideal, we avoid."12. In a nutshell Ramakrishna meant: "As many faiths, so many paths."

SWAMI VIVEKANANDA

His admirers and devotees in the global Vedanta community lovingly refer to him as Swamiji. He was born on January 12, 1863 in Calcutta and was given the name Naren. From the outset of his life he had a natural inclination toward skepticism – perhaps the sign of a healthy, inquiring mind. He would not accept religion on the grounds of mere faith; he wanted a demonstration of God. Christopher Isherwood gives us a portrait of young Naren's character, the product of a Western education. "[He was] a highly skeptical young man with a Western agnostic education in Calcutta, who refused utterly to believe in the supernormal until he had, so to speak, banged his head against it, and even when Vivekananda's disbelief had been modified by personal experience, even when he had become one of Ramakrishna's most passionate devotees, he still discouraged blind faith in others, still urged everyone to find out the truth for himself. And, over and over again, he asserted that it really did not matter whether you believed that Ramakrishna was a divine incarnation or not. Can we accuse such men of lying?"13.

At 18 years of age, after joining the Bramo Samaj sect, and unfulfilled, Naren met Ramakrishna at Dakshineswar. But Swamiji's skepticism remained unabated by his encounter with Ramakrishna because he could not accept the idea that he and his Creator were one and the same. But Ramakrishna's patience was inexhaustible. He put his young disciple through a round of encounters with the nature of spiritual reality – experiences that any other disciple would have given his eyeteeth for, but this was not proof enough for young Naren who remained intransigent in his doubt. "One day at the temple garden he laughingly said to a friend: 'How silly! This jug is God! This cup is God. Whatever we see is God! And we too are God! Nothing could be more absurd!' Sri Ramakrishna came out of his room and gently touched him. Spellbound, he immediately perceived that everything was indeed God. A new universe opened around him. Returning home in a dazed state, he found there too that the food, the plate, the eater himself, the people around him were all God. When he walked in the street, he saw that the cabs, the horses, the streams of people, the buildings, were all Brahman. He could hardly go about his day's business. His parents became anxious about him and thought he was ill. And when the intensity of the experience abated a little, he saw the world as a dream. Walking in the public square, he would strike his head against the iron fences to know whether they were real. It took him a number of days to recover his normal self. He had a foretaste of the great experiences yet to come and felt that the words of Vedanta were true."14.

Vivekananda puts his experience in his own words. "One day in the temple garden at Dakshineswar, Shri Ramakrishna touched me over the heart, and first of all I began to see that the houses, rooms, doors, windows, verandahs – the trees, the sun, the moon – all were flying off, shattering to pieces as it were – reduced to atoms and molecules – and ultimately became merged in the Akasha [the material comprising everything in the universe]. Gradually again, the Akasha also vanished, and after that, my consciousness of the ego with it. What happened next I do not recollect. I was at first frightened. Coming back from that state again I began to see the houses, doors, windows, verandahs, and other things. On another occasion, I had exactly the same realization by the side of a lake in America."15.

Disciples and devotees of Ramakrishna base their faith on his being the avatar of the age on a significant criterion: he was able to transmit Nirvikalpa samadhi (the highest realization of God or Divine Union in a Christian sense) by means of touch or even a glance. Only an incarnation, they maintain, possesses that power. A prophet, a saint, or even a realized guru can only point the way based on his or her own experience. Or in some cases can lift an individual's kundalini (serpent or spiritual power lying at the base of the spine in every human being) awakening him or her temporarily. A case in point is the following example. When Ramakrishna was on his deathbed, he climbed off his mattress and bestowed samadhi to his inner circle of devotees, who had arrived at his bedside to pay their final respects. Writes his astonished Chronicler M, "Then Ramakrishna stood up, forgetting all about his painful and fatal illness. The doctor, who had been sitting in front of him, also stood up. Both patient and physician forgot themselves in the spell created by Narendra's music. The younger Naren and Latu went into deep samadhi. The atmosphere of the room became electric. Everyone felt the presence of God. Dr. Sarkar, eminent scientist that he was, stood breathless, watching this strange scene. He noticed that the devotees who had gone into samadhi were utterly unconscious of the outer world. All were motionless and transfixed. After a while as they came down a little to the plane of the relative world, some laughed and some wept."16.

Besides being instrumental in laying the groundwork for a future Vedanta movement in India, Vivekananda brought Ramakrishna's teachings to the West. And his message of Vedanta to Westerners could be put neatly into a nutshell, and if they could not remember much of what he told them, they should never forget that, "You're not to become pure, you're pure already. You're not to become perfect, you're that already." In Ramakrishna's view the young Naren was selected for this very purpose. Ramakrishna, therefore, could not allow Swamiji to remain long in samadhi, because he would remain in it for the duration of his life and never accomplish his mission. Ramakrishna stated metaphorically, "I have locked him in the room and kept the key." And he asked his Divine Mother, "Mother, entangle him in Maya; otherwise he will give up his body in samadhi."17.

"After another long period, Narendra [Vivekananda] regained full consciousness. Bathed in peace, he went to the Master, who said: 'now the Mother has shown you everything. But this revelation will remain under lock and key, and I shall keep the key. When you have accomplished the Mother's work you will find the treasure again.'"18.

While Vivekananda concentrated his focus on the "Self" and its oneness with the universe in his message to the West, he extended a large priority toward bringing Ramakrishna's ideal of spiritual harmony to audiences segregated by denominations. Speaking at the Parliament of Religions before a delegation representing many of the world's creeds, in Chicago in 1893, the Swami separated his idea of ecumenicalism into three categories: intolerance. tolerance and acceptance. He spoke about intolerance, "Sectarianism, bigotry, and its horrible descendant, fanaticism, have long possessed this beautiful earth. They have filled the earth with violence, drenched it often and often with human blood, destroyed civilization and sent whole nations to despair. Had it not been for these horrible demons, human society would be far more advanced than it is now. But their time is come; and I fervently hope that the bell that tolled this morning in honor of this convention may be the death-knell of all fanaticism, of all persecutions with the sword or with the pen, between persons wending their way to the same goal."19.

His second topic was tolerance – a kind of coexistence, leading in some cases to ecumenical exchanges whereby "interfaith" conferences and meetings are convened, but partisan smugness remains among many attendees. Vivekananda held India up as the example, having made a practice of this attitude centuries before when religious feuding placed each sect at the other's throat elsewhere. "I am proud to belong to a nation which has sheltered the persecuted and the refugees of all religions and nations of the earth. I am proud to tell you that we have gathered to our bosom the purest remnant of the Israelites, who came to Southern India and took refuge with us in the very year in which their holy temple was shattered to pieces by Roman tyranny. I am proud to belong to the religion which has sheltered and is still fostering the remnant of the grand Zoroastrian nation. I will quote to you, brethren, a few lines from a hymn which I remember from my earliest boyhood, which is every day repeated by millions of human beings: 'As the different streams having their sources in different places all mingle their water in the sea, so O Lord, the different paths which men take through different tendencies, various through they appear, crooked or straight, all lead to thee."20.

When acceptance arrives all religions embrace one another as their own. Vivekananda called this attitude the "Temple Universal" and believed all religions are struggling consciously or unconsciously to find this unity. "If there is ever to be a universal religion, it must be one which will have no location in place or time; which will be infinite like the God it will preach, and whose sun will shine upon the followers of Krishna and of Christ, on saints and sinners alike; which will not be Brahminic or Buddhistic, Christian or Mohammedan, but the sum total of all these, and still have infinite space for development; which in its Catholicity will embrace in its infinite arms, and find a place for every human being, from the lowest groveling savage not far removed from the brute, to the highest man towering by the virtues of his head and heart almost above humanity, making society stand in awe of him and doubt his human nature. It will be a religion which will have no place for persecution or intolerance in its polity, which will recognize divinity in every man and woman, and whose whole scope, whose whole force, will be created in aiding humanity to realise its own true, divine nature."21.

SRI SARADA DEVI

After Ramakrishna passed away in 1886, his disciples gathered around him and, "Latter in the dark, came a woman, sitting at his feet crying softly, and calling him 'Mother.' It was that disciple who had been his wife."22.

Known to her devotees the world over as the "Holy Mother," Sarada Devi was the spiritual wife of Ramakrishna, but not in the sense of the ordinary householder, for their relationship was one of untainted purity. During the lifetime of Ramakrishna, the Holy Mother lived a life of complete self-effacement in background seclusion, while serving him and his devotees hand-and-foot. This was not out of inconsiderate male chauvinism on Ramakrishna's part, but was based on her own volition. For thirty-four years after Ramakrishna passed away, she carried on his earthly ministry, leading many souls to God and liberation. Once Sarada's mother asked the Paramahamsa about the childless gap in her daughter's life. Ramakrishna responded that Sarada would have so many children that she would be tired of being called Mother. And so the Holy Mother was the mother to broods of "her children" who sought her divinity and spiritual guidance. The Holy Mother initiated everyone who approached her sincerely, and even the lukewarm she called her children, too. The Mother had a special compassion for ruffians and miscreants. When waylaid by the Bagdi robbers, she responded, "I am your daughter, Sarada," and from that moment they became as her own parents.

Holy Mother's contribution to Temple Universal was her large heart – there was no one she did not accept as her "Children." The Mother's heart pierced through caste and religious denomination – and even extended to individuals of dubious virtue who sought her help. One such person was Amjad, a reputed robber of the Muslim faith. Amjad met the Mother at her ashram in Jayrambati, and he became her disciple. He was inclined to arrive at her cottage with offerings of vegetables. Amjad, a humble youth approached her hesitantly, but after receiving her affectionate welcome, which was her custom of making offerings to her "children" with the saying, "Come my child, here is pradsad for you," the boy loosened up before the others of her household and accepted what she had to offer.

Amjad was hired to build the wall for the Mother's new cottage in Jayrambati. As everyone was treated equally as her "child," she invited him for a meal on the porch of her house. This did not sit well with some members of her household, devout Hindus, who eyed the Muslim as an untouchable and regarded any food or drink touched by him as polluted. Observes Swami Nikhilananda, "Nalini, Holy Mother's niece, began to throw the food at Amjad's plate from a distance. Holy Mother noticed this and said: 'How can one enjoy food if it is offered with such scorn? Let me wait on him properly.' After he had finished his meal, Holy Mother cleaned the place with her own hands, Nalini shrieked: 'Aunt, you have lost your caste!' 'Keep quiet,' the Mother scolded her and she added: 'As Sarat [Swami Saradananda] is my son, exactly so is Amjad!' Her mode of equitable conduct upon this occasion justifies her remark, 'I am the Mother of the good and I am the Mother of the wicked.'"23.

On another occasion, the Mother told off a namby-pamby monk, a resident of the Udbodham House (Holy Mother's residence in Calcutta), who was upset over the presence of certain women reputed to be of low moral character, who visited the house from time to time. The Mother chided the straight-laced monk, "If they are prevented from coming here, I will leave this place."24.

Even after she had reached the summit of her role of teacher and guru, the Holy Mother still immersed herself in the drudgeries of domestic chores, and her closest devotees were taken aback by seeing her in the role of a servant in her own household. Many people harbored doubts about her tenacity of renunciation. One such person, Yogin-Ma, a close associate and confidant, received a vision of Ramakrishna, who set her straight on the matter. "Look here," he remarked with a stentorious bark, "can anything ever make the Ganges impure? Can anything defile its waters? Regard her (Holy Mother) too in the same way. Never have any doubt about her. Know that she and this (referring to himself) are identical." 25.

Ramakrishna saw the Divine Mother in Sarada. When asked by her, "How do you look on me?" Out came the reply, "The Mother who is in the temple, the Mother who has given birth to this body, and is now living in the nahabat – the same Mother is now massaging my feet. Truly, I always look upon you as a form of the blissful divine Mother."26.

One swami recalls that Holy Mother admitted to him that she was the Mother of all, even of these birds and animals."27.

Introduction

Behind the naturalistic religion of the North American Red Man is the chief aim of self-realization. The goal of many Native Americans is the same as that of Eastern mysticism – Self-realization while still in the human physical body. Writes Orientalist and editor of the Tibetan Book of the Dead, Evans Wentz, "The fundamental doctrine of the Naturalistic religion of the Red men seem to have arisen as a direct outcome of self-realization, in the Hindu meaning of self-realization, born of yogic practices peculiarly American but akin, in some instances, to those of the Hindu and Tibetans. In other words, the non-Christianized Red Men believe only that which they realize through their own psychic experiences, mainly in dreams and in the disembodied state of 'astral- body' projections. They cannot comprehend any religion divorced from such psychic experiences and based upon mere belief."[1]. The cardinal belief of Siouan spirituality is that every action he makes is a religious act, the same spirit in all creation is central and from this he or she draws spiritual power.

Akin to Advaita Vedanta (non-dual) God is not Everything, but Everything is God. Ramakrishna supports this contention. "The scriptures say that whatever you see in the world is truly one nondual Brahman, be it gross or subtle, sentient or insentient, bricks, wood, clay, stone, trees, plants, human beings, animals, gods, or demigods. You are seeing, hearing, touching, smelling, and tasting the same Brahman in various forms and in different states."2.

Lakota medicine man, Lame Deer, gives us the Lakota's Advaita perception. "We Indians live in a world of symbols and images where the spiritual and the commonplace are one. To you symbols are just words or a written book. To us they are part of nature, part of ourselves – the earth, the sun, the wind and the rain, stones, trees, animals, even little insects like ants and grasshoppers. We try to understand them not with the head but with the heart, and we need no more than a hint to give us the meaning."3.

Brahman to the Indian is the same as the Great Spirit. Lame Deer explains, "The Great Spirit is one, yet he is many. He is part of the sun and the sun is part of him. He can be in a thunder bird or in an animal or plant."4.

Santee Sioux spokesperson, Ohiyesa, puts it this way, [The Indian child from early on], "thinks that he is a blood brother to all living creatures, and the storm wind is to him a messenger of the 'Great Mystery.'"5.

There are some misconceptions of the term "Sioux". Older generations of Lakota found the word inoffensive and identified themselves with the name. As younger generations became more politically conscious the term took on a negative connotation, even a derogatory meaning. Some contemporary activist even take issue with the meaning of Oglala. According to Luther Standing Bear, the famous holy man who narrated his biography in 1932, The Land of the

Spotted Eagle, "The word Oglala conveys the idea of being covered over with dust or ashes and this is how the word came to be applied to a band [tribe]."6.

After the reservation was established, the agent found it inconvenient to have so many bands in his six districts, so the Pine Ridge Reservation called all the bands Oglala. Oglala is one of the sub tribes of the Teton or Western Sioux.

In their book, Walking in the Sacred Manner, Mark St. Pierre and Tilda Long Soldier have gone a long was to clear up the misconception of this issue. "The term Sioux is misleading because it has no specific reference within Lakota people's history. They call themselves Sioux when giving their tribe name to non-Indians but call themselves Lakota, which means "the Allies." Sioux is said to be a shortening of an Ojibway word, Naddowissi ("lesser snakes," "adders," or "enemy".) with the French plural – IOUX, thus becoming Naddowissi , which was shortened over time to Sioux.

"In a real sense Sioux refers to all tribes of the lose confederation known as the Oceti Sakowin or Seven Council Fires. Within this confederation (which may have been more philosophical than actual) were three main divisions, the Dakota, Nakota, and Lakota. Each of the three major subdivisions is characterized by differences in dialect and to some extent, cultural orientation. [Lakota is the language of the Oglala]. The Dakota were woodlands or Park Lands people with ties to other Woodlands tribes, sharing some of their cosmology and worldview. The Nakota occupied a vast territory east of the Missouri River and shared traits with other river peoples, such as agriculture and occasionally earth lodges (Drifting Goose band). The Lakota had in common with other high plains' peoples a unique religious and philosophical system, including the Sun Dance and Vision Quest. "The Dakota (eastern division) comprised four "seats" – the Mide Wakanton, (Spirit Lake people), the Wakpe' Kute" (Shooters Among the Leaves), Sissitoin (Fish-Scale Dwellers), and Whapeton (Leaf Dwellers). These Dakota people live today on various reservations in South Dakota, North Dakota, Minnesota, Montana, and Canada.

" The Nakota (middle) comprised the two Ihanktowan or Yankton (End Dwellers) groups, which occupied two "seats" on the mythical councils.

The final group and the group which most of the information in this book (Walking in the Sacred Manner) comes are the Lakota. Although in earlier times they occupied only one "seat" in the Seven Council Fires, they eventually grew in strength and numbers. By 1775 they had crossed the Missouri River and became subdivided into seven tribes themselves. Within that time frame they acquired the horse and became the buffalo hunting warriors of legend.

"These bands or tribes from the largest to smallest, are as follows: the Oglala, on the Pine Ridge Reservation in South Dakota; the Sicangu (Brule), on Rosebud and Lower Brule Reservations in South Dakota; and the Minnecojou (Plants by the Water Peoples).

" The Hunkpapa (Camps at the Horn, Sitting Bull's people) live in the South Dakota portion of the Standing Rock Reservation near McLaughlin, South Dakota. The Itazipco, (Sans Arc, or Bowless Band), who are the traditional keepers of the Sacred Pipe, live along the Moreau River on the Cheyenne River Reservation.

"The two smallest groups, largely intermarried today, are the O-ohe' nunpa (Two Kettle), on the east end of the Cheyenne River, and the Si Sapa or Black feet Sioux, living in the northeastern part of the Cheyenne River Reservation and on Standing Rock.

"The Lakota constitute by far the largest Sioux population today, numbering some seventy thousand."7.

The band names Lakota/Oglala are used interchangeably in this book, and the word "Sioux" is used as a generic term to cover the discussion of the seven bands constituting the Sioux nation.

The principle narrators found in our discussion are mostly Lakota and were practitioners of traditional medicine – shamans or medicine men and were venerated as holy men by tribal members and non-Indians who compiled their biographies in the form of personal interviews.

There were three Black Elks among the Lakota. Nick Black Elk was the subject of John Neihardt's Black Elk Speaks (1932). Ben Black Elk, Nick's son, translated Nick's narrative to Enid, Neihardt's daughter, who actually took in shorthand, the field notes from which the book was created. Wallace Black Elk also said to be an holy man and a notable shaman, authored, Black Elk, The Sacred Ways of a Lakota, co-authored and translated by William Lyon in 1990. Black Elk's spiritual name was Little Eagle.

In 1948, Nick Black Elk had reached the end of his life and collaborated with Joseph Epes Brown – The Sacred Pipe, 1953, because, "he did not wish that this sacred lore, much of which he alone knew should pass with him."

Nick Black Elk and Luther Standing Bear were old enough to remember Custer's Last Stand. Both men spoke at length about roaming the wide open plains in pursuit of the buffalo as free Sioux before the tragedy of being placed in designated areas, their buffalo almost extinct, their sacred religion forbidden even within the circumscribed boundaries of the reservation.

Much less reserved and up-to-date are two members of the Lakota people: Lame Deer and Wallace Black Elk, who were unapologetically Sioux, but have somewhat assimilated in to the trappings of a hip, non-Indian culture of the mid twentieth century. A quote from Wallace Black Elk is a case in point. "People have a false sense of security with no comprehension of the spirit powers. One time someone said to me in an educated way, 'Well, experience is the best teacher.' So I asked, 'Well, who is that 'teacher.' Anyway? Is it Budweiser?" Black Elk is prone to laugh at himself. Some of his statements and "hogie pogie" practices have left him vulnerable to ridicule. Many rational-minded people after delving into the mysteries and experiences of shamans, such as Black Elk's have frequently scoffed at the evidence (of the sacred ceremonies) as unbelievable in their terms, but in Black Elk's view, to laugh them away is to give these medicine people the last laugh.

On the other hand, Vine Deloria, God is Red, himself an Oglala, and spokesperson, lawyer and professor of Native American Studies, finds Lame Deer laudable. Lame Deer produced a, "saucy style, typical of the well-experienced Sioux elder making cynical but incisive comments on human behavior. Readers accustomed to the pious Protestant tracts on the devotional life [of the Indians] were shocked at Lame Deer's casual approach to such taboo subjects as death, sex, growing old, and religion. Yet from the pages of the book shone a wisdom found in few devotional materials."8.

Another major contributor is Leonard Crow Dog, also a Lakota medicine man; somewhat more contemporary than the others (b. 1942) supplies us with humorous anecdotes of four generations of tribal medicine men, his ancestors. Leonard is also noted for his involvement within the American Indian Movement (AIM), the Native American counterpart of the Civil Rights movement of the nineteen sixties. Leonard was not only the spiritual leader in the Indian's demand for self-determination, but was responsible for the renewal of the banned Ghost Dance.

The Creation Myth

Standing Bear states his version of the Lakota matrix: one morning a lone man awoke and emerged from the soil. In the sunlight the man was unable to see the natural configuration of the mountains; the only thing he saw was soft quaking mud, for the planet was new. The man stumbled about; the sun was pivotal in creating the beautiful scenario of the region. And from this arose the Lakota nation, and was never shared with any other nation until the coming of the European. The bigger miracle, according to Standing Bear, was the conception not the birth; few can guess what goes on underground before a flower pushes through the dirt. Says Standing Bear, "We are of the soil and the soil is of us. We love the birds and beasts that grew with us on this soil. They drank the same water we did and breathed the same air. We are all one in nature. Believing so, there was in our hearts a great peace and a welling kindness for all living, growing things."1.

Mark St. Pierre and Tilda Long Soldier tell a tale of Iyan, the rock that existed in a dark and lonely void. Iyan desired to create something in its place, so no longer would he be lonely, and so he would be able to expand his power over something else beside himself. He pierced himself, and his blood, which was blue, flowed out until he was shriveled hard, and powerless. What came from him formed maka Ina (Mother Earth). The blue also formed the oceans, but the powers released could not reside in the water, so they formed the blue sky dome and called it Mahpiyato (blue sky). In Lakota belief Inyan was the first physical being. Lame Deer internalizes, "Sometimes I feel like the first being in one of our Indian legends. This was a giant made of earth, water, the moon and winds. He had timber instead of hair, a whole forest of trees. He had a huge lake in his stomach and a waterfall in his crotch. I feel like this giant. All of nature is in me, and a bit of myself is in all of nature."2.

The humans followed Iyan, the people Standing Bear referred to who dwelled beneath the surface of the earth, and were created to serve the gods. They were called Pte'oyate' or Buffalo Nation, and they became the Lakota. Their chief was Wazi (Old Man), and his wife was called Wakanka or Old Woman.

Camelot

Standing Bear speaks of the serene Oglala landscape, still an Eden at the time of his birth. "I began my life amid a scene of natural harmony where youthful life had happy care and direction from all the tribe, where maturity was gladdened with health, generosity in act and spirit, and strength from the unlimited source, and where old age looked calmly to a future of security and peace."1.

For the Lakota nature was not dangerous but hospitable, not forbidding but friendly. Nature infused itself inside the Indian so as to be fathomed by him. Standing Bear honors the ecology enjoyed by the first Lakota right up to the coming of the European who preempted it. "We did not think of the great open plains, the beautiful rolling hills and winding streams with tangled growth as 'wild'. Only to the white man was nature a 'wilderness,' and only to him was the land 'infested' with 'wild' animals and 'savage' people. To us it was tame. Earth was bountiful and we were surrounded with the blessings of the Great Mystery. Not until the hairy man from the east came and with brutal frenzy heaped injustices upon us and the families that we loved was it 'wild' for us. When the very animals of the forest began fleeing from his approach, then it was for us the 'Wild West' began."2.

Swami Vivekananda echoes Standing Bear's insights; with enlightened sarcasm he points out the relativity of progress, a Western obsession. " 'A good world', 'a happy world', and 'social progress', are all terms equally intelligible, with 'hot ice' or 'dark light.' If it were good, it would not be the world. The soul foolishly thinks of manifesting the Infinite in finite matter, Intelligence through gross particles; but at last it finds out its error and tries to escape. This going back is the beginning of religion, and its method, destruction of self, that is love. Not love for wife or child or anybody else, except this little self. Never be deluded by the tall talk, of which you will hear so much in America, about 'human progress' and such stuff. There is no progress without corresponding digression. In one society there is one set of evils; in another, another. So with periods of history. In the Middle Ages, there were more robbers, now more cheats. At one period there is less idea of married life; at another more prostitution. In one more physical agony; in another, a thousand-fold more mental. So with knowledge. Did not gravitation already exist in Nature before it was observed and named? Then what difference does it make to know that it exists? Are you happier than the Red Indians?"3.

In the Lakota concept science and religion were not separate but both one.

Lame Deer sums up the Sioux ideal. "We would find again the flowering prairie unspoiled with herds of buffalo and antelope, its clouds of birds, belonging to everyone, enjoyed by all."4.

This idea of an idyllic Eden before humankind gathered in cities and was ruled by kings, emperors, dictators, papal counsels, and multinational corporations was found widespread throughout the world. In India there was the ideal of the Swaraj: every village had its own rule. The wistful memory of classical India, a pastoral memory of a time just out of reach, when people knew the undefiled gods, and the gods gave the Brahmans all the answers, and the bull drew the plough, and the cow gave milk, and the manure of these animals enriched the fields, and the stalks of the harvest thatched the simple huts of the pure.

William Prescott, notable authority of Pre-Columbian America cites the idyllic Tula, capital of the classical Toltecs in the golden age under the reign of Topiltzin Quetzalcoatl. "In that land the crop of maize never failed, and the ears grew as long as a man's arm; the cotton burst its pods, not white only, but naturally of all beautiful colors, scarlet green, blue, orange, what you would; the gourds could not be clasped in the arms; birds of beauteous plumage filled the air with melodious song. There was never any want or poverty. All the riches of the world were there, houses built of silver and precious jade, of rosy mother of pearl and azure turquoise." 5.

Sarada Devi, the Holy Mother explains why these utopias could not endure – it was due to the gunas: Tamas, Rajas, and Sattva, the tendencies which make up all of nature and the universe. One of her devotees cites an interview he had with her. In the course of the conversation, she said, "At the time of creation, people were born with the quality of Sattva, light. They had wisdom from their very birth. Consequently they at once realized the unreal nature of the world. They renounced it and practiced austerity. They were liberated in no time. The Creator found that the purpose of His creation was going to be frustrated. These wise men, who were thus liberated, were unfit for the continuance of the play of the world. Then He again started the work of creation and mixed the qualities of Rajas (activity) and Tamas (inertia) with the Sattva. Thus His purpose was fulfilled."6.

The concept of the gunas is one of the most complex tenets of Vedanta philosophy. Swami Vivekananda makes them more comprehensible to the reader in his own concise way. "According to Yoga philosophy, the whole of nature consists of three qualities or forces; one is called Tamas, another Rajas, and the third Sattva. These three qualities manifest themselves in the physical world as darkness or inactivity, attraction or repulsion, and equilibrium of the two. Everything that is in nature, all manifestations, are combinations and recombinations of these three forces."7. If a person is dominated by one or the other his or her nature is characterized.

The Great Spirit

The Lakota does not pray to Wakan-Tanka (Tunkashila). Yet he or she realizes that Wakan-Tanka controls the universe. The attitude of the Sioux and indeed many tribes of the plains toward Wakan-Tanka is that He or She is like the Christian Trinity – a mystery of many persons in one. Sword of the Oglala explains, "Every object in the world has a spirit and that spirit is Wakan. Thus the spirit of the tree or things of that kind, while not like the spirit of man, are also Wakan. Wakan comes from Wakan beings. These Wakan beings are greater than mankind in the same way that mankind is greater than animals. They are never born and they never die. They can do many things that mankind cannot do. Mankind can pray to the Wakan beings for help. There are many of these beings but are four kinds. The word

Wankan-Tanka means all of the Wakan beings, because they are all as if one. Wakan-Tanka Kin signifies the chief or leading Wakan being which is the Sun. However, the most powerful of the Wakan beings is Nagi-Tanka, the Great Spirit who is also Tanku Skanskan. Taku Skanskan signifies the Blue, in other words the Sky…Mankind is permitted to pray to the Wakan beings. If their prayer is directed to all the good Wakan beings, they should pray to Wakan Tanka; but if the prayer is offered to only one of these beings, then the one addressed should be named …Wakan Tanka is like sixteen different persons; but each person is Kan. Therefore, they are all only the same as one."1.

Chased-by-Bears of the Dakota points out that Wakan-Tanka is near yet far, but remains unknown. "We are sure that he hears us, and yet it is hard to explain what we believe about this…We believe that he is everywhere, yet he is to us as the spirit of our (dead) friends, whose voices we cannot hear."2.

Contemporary Lakota refer to Wakan-Tanka as the superior deity, one comparable to the Creator God, who is the primary, supernatural unifying force. A beautiful passage expressed by Standing Bear, not only sums up Wakan-Tanka, but rings a familiar non-dual Vedanta cord. "From Wakan-Tanka there came a great unifying life force that flowed in and through all things…the flowers of the plains, blowing winds, rocks, trees, birds, animals…And was the same force that had been breathed into the first man. Thus all things were kindred and brought together by the same Great Mystery."3. What Standing Bear was referring to is Prana, the vital life force that permeates everything in the universe. We will encounter this topic in a further chapter.

The One As Many: Advaita

The Lakota and Vivekananda express an Advaita idea: God is not Everything but Everything is God. Says Swamiji, "That the explanation of the thing comes from within itself is still more completely satisfied by Vedanta. The Brahman, the God of the Vedanta has nothing outside of Himself; nothing at all. All this indeed is He: He is in the universe: He is the universe Himself. 'Thou art the man, Thu art the woman, Thou art the young man walking in the pride of youth, Thou art the old man tottering in his step.' He is here. Him we see and feel: in Him we live and move, and have our being. You have that conception in the New Testament. It is that idea, God immanent in the universe, the very essence, the heart, the soul of things. He manifests Himself, as it were, in this universe. You and I are little bits, little points, little channels, little expressions, all living inside of that infinite ocean of Existence, Knowledge, and Bliss. The difference between man and man and animals, between plants and stones is not in kind, because everyone from the highest angel, to the lowest particle of matter is but an expression of that one infinite ocean, and the difference is only in degree. I am a low manifestation, you may be a higher, but in both the materials are the same. You and I are both outlets of the same channel, and that is God."1.

Advaita evolved out of the grasp of the most primitive dualism – that is humankind and God are separate. The modern school of non-dual Vedanta embraces the concept of the deity, which declares that God is everything or finally everything is God. Vivekananda traces the evolution of humankind's spirituality in relation to God. "The religions of the unthinking masses all over the world teach, and have always taught, of a God who is outside the universe, who lives in heaven, who governs from a place, who is the punisher of the bad and rewarder of the good, and so on. As man advances spiritually, he begins to feel that God is omnipresent, that he must be in him, that He must be everywhere, that He is not a distant God, but clearly the Soul of all souls. As my soul moves my body, even so is God the mover of my soul – the soul within the soul. And a few individuals of pure heart and highly developed mind go still farther, and at last find God, as the New Testament says: 'Blessed are the pure in heart, for they shall see God.' And they find at last that they and the Father are one."2. Or to explain what "That man in Gethsemane" realized, "the infinite is one and not many, and the one Infinite Soul is reflecting Itself through thousands and thousands of mirrors, appearing as so many different souls. It is the same Infinite Soul, which is the background of the universe, that

THE ONE AS MANY: ADVAITA

we call God. The same Infinite Soul also is the background of the human mind, which we call the human soul."3.

Nick Black Elk expresses the idea that the human being is a totality and the universe is within him/herself. "Peace comes within the souls of men, when they realize that their relationship, their oneness with the universe and all its powers, and when they realize that at the center of the universe dwells Wakan-Tanka, and that this center is really everywhere, it is within each of us."4.

The Santee Sioux's temple is entirely conceived within the idea of naturalism; no formal temple is needed to separate the devotee from nature since both are God. Comments Ohiyesa, "Being a natural man, the Indian was intensely poetical. He would deem it a sacrilege to build a house for Him who may be met face to face in the mysterious shadowy aisles of the primeval forest, or on the sunlit bosom of virgin prairies, upon dizzying spires and pinnacles of naked rock, and yonder in the jeweled vault of the night sky. He who enrobes Himself in filmy veils of cloud, there on the rim of the visible world where our Great-Grandfather Sun kindles his evening campfire. He who rides upon the rigorous wind of the north, or breathes forth His spirit upon aromatic southern airs, whose war canoe is launched upon majestic rivers and inland seas, needs no lesser cathedral."5.

The Great Mystery

One of the most appealing aspects that the religion of the Vedas uses to tantalize the interest of the Western mind is its absolute rational conception of the universe. Rather than undergoing a formal creation or genesis by the fiat of some deistic superman of which many dualistic theologians espouse, because a medieval edict argued that metaphysical abstractions are too intricate for the minds of the laity, the Vedantin conceives of an infinite universe existing throughout eternity – only after eons it involves and then after more eons it evolves – the kalpa –with neither a Beginning nor End. Simply put it always was/is.

The idea of time leads us to naturally assume a beginning and with a beginning a subsequent ending. Vivekananda says that which is created has a beginning and an end – linear time, but the universe was never created. No concept of time is possible - i.e., maya. Both Vedantins and many Native Americans see such a notion (beginning and end) as an illusion. Instead the Sioux believe that anything created must fall into dissolution, but the universe was never created, therefore, it will never be destroyed. Thus, this answer is given to agnostics who ask, "Who created God?" God is inseparable from the universe. Ramakrishna uses the metaphor of the spider and its web: Brahman is like a spider who projects its web out of itself and then becomes immersed in it; and so death is impossible for God and for that matter any form of material being, from an atom to a human is God (differing not in kind but in degree, the atom will evolve through myriads of bodies in which myriads of experiences will enlarge its consciousness until it reaches the body of a perfect God man and is liberated, never to be reborn again), the infinite, incapable of being destroyed, because how can the infinite be annihilated? answers the Advaitist. The atman (Soul or real Self) pervading all sentient beings, and for that matter everything in the universe – for (as we shall discover) even a rock has consciousness – likewise cannot be extinguished, because it is the real nature of Brahman/ Wakan Tanka, outside of time, without beginning or end, and never created because it always was.

Yet the universe is not like some stagnant pond sitting forever as moss and scum collect at its outer rim. It has its lila (play) as it were. The lila being a cycle of involution and evolution. During the former Brahman/Wakan-Tanka (the absolute) absorbs all of creation unto His/Herself, and then after a period of inestimable time –since time itself is absorbed – the latter takes place – the whole cycle is reversed, and all of creation unfolds again. The Vedanta calls this Naha Yuga – the entire universe passes into a superannuated state at the end of a kalpa or great cycle, and then comes forth again. There is the rhythm of created power in the kalpa – sometimes compared to a microcosmic breathing, called in Vedanta Pravrtti (in-out) or the universe in involution, and Nivrtti when it returns to evolution or becomes evolved. The sum total of these breaths (or cycles) makes up eternity.

Vivekananda's rational interpretation is that, "The question may be asked, how was it at the first cycle? The answer is what is the meaning of a first cycle? There was none. If you can give a beginning to time, the whole concept of time will be destroyed. Try to think of a limit where time began, you have to think of time beyond that limit. Try to think where space begins, you will have to think of space beyond that. Time and space are infinite, and therefore have neither beginning nor end. This is a better idea than that God created the universe in five minutes and then went to sleep and since then has been sleeping."1.

The Great Mystery contains the idea that creation was predicated on God's breath. This is closely analogous to the Vedanta concept which compares the kalpa to the continuous inhaling and exhaling in the human body. Says Swami Vivekananda, "The universe as it were, is being breathed out of Him and again it shrinks into Him and again He throws it out."2.

Many American Indians symbolize the breath of life ceremoniously: the smoking of tobacco, the dispersal of Holy corn-pollen to symbolize fruitfulness and productivity, and by planting plumed prayer-sticks upon feathers of which he breathes, the prayer can be carried to the Great Spirit on the wind. The prayer-sticks serve a similar function to the prayer flags of the Buddhist Tibetans.

The Native Americans do not speak of the beginning. According to John Collier, U.S. commissioner of Indian

Affairs (1933-1945): "They [the Indians] know nothing of the beginning, nor will they say that there is a hell. They cannot conceive of such a thing. They say this: That men must follow the right path of living. They must live according to the laws of nature which are moral laws. If they fail to do that they hurt themselves and that is all the punishment there is. They point to the Milky Way, which has a branch leading off into emptiness. If a man fails to live according to the laws of nature, he goes off on that side branch which ends in emptiness."3.

In the Ojibway creation myth, the Great Spirit created two cranes – male and female – who settled upon an environment where the supply of fish was inexhaustible. Hence, they made their home and the world came into being.

"Once while roaming through a field, Gadadhar [Ramakrishna] saw a beautiful black cloud heavy with rain; against it flew a flock of cranes, rhythmically spreading their white wings. He was so captivated by this sight that he completely lost awareness of his body and the objects of this world and fell unconscious on a ridge in the field."4.

The Lakota have their own charming interpretation: at the center of their involution theory is the buffalo. In the beginning of a cycle –creation – a buffalo is placed in the west in order to hold back the waters. Every year the buffalo sheds a hair, and in every age (four ages) he loses a leg. When all his hair and all four legs are gone, the waters pour over everything and the cycle comes to an end. The poem of the Arrca (Inca) warrior explains how the sun died. "Long ago the sun is said to have died. For five days after its death, it was night. The stones began to jostle each other, the mortars large and small began to eat people, the pestles too."5.

Swamiji compares the Lakota's Buffalo to ebullit bubbles in a kettle of boiling water whereby everything in the universe is reabsorbed into Brahman and escapes its incarnate bondage after eons. Then after incalculable time a new cycle will be recapitulated. "In time to come Christs will be born in numbers like bunches of grapes on a vine; then the play will be over and all will pass out – as water in a kettle beginning to boil shows first one bubble, then another, then more and more, until all is in ebullition and passes out as steam. Buddha and Christ are the two biggest bubbles the world has yet produced. Moses was a tiny bubble; greater and greater came. Sometime, however, all will be bubbles and escape. But Creation ever new, will bring new water to go through the process all over again."6.

The Atman

There is an Oglala version of the Atman or soul closely parallel to that of Vedanta. "Anything that has a birth will have a death; souls are unborn and consequently do not die."1.

The basis of all non-dual religion is self-realization that argues that the unchanging Atman is none other than Brahman His/Herself. Vivekananda observes that the Atman is nowhere in circumference, but who's center is everywhere or infinity itself. Says the Swami, "None comes and none goes, says the non-dualist. How can you come and go? You are infinite. Where is the place for you to go? In a certain school a number of little children were being examined... Among others there was this question, 'Why does not the earth fall...But one bright little girl answered it with another question – 'Where shall it fall?' The very question of the examiner was nonsense on the face of it. There is no up and down in the universe; the idea is only relative. So it is with regard to the soul; the very question of birth and death in regard to it is utter nonsense. Who goes and who comes? Where are you not? Where is the heaven that you are not in already? Omnipresent is the Self of man. Where is it to go? Where is it not to go? It is everywhere."2.

Maya, The Great Deceiver

The Vedic understanding of maya is that this world is unreal; it is only a mere appearance. Swami Vivekananda holds that the Vedantic view is "[A] world [which] has no existence. What is meant by that? It means that it has no absolute existence. It exists only in relation to my mind, to your mind, and to the mind of everyone else. We see this world with five senses, but if we had another sense, we would see something more. If we had yet another sense, it would appear as something still different. It has, therefore, no real existence; it has no unchangeable, immovable infinite existence. Nor can it be called non-existence, seeing that it exists, and we have to work in and through it. It is a mixture of existence and non-existence."1.

The real world, according to the Lakota and the Sioux, is not the one of appearances perceived by the rational secular mind, but one that can only be reached through spiritual practice, the one we can be taught to "see" and experience. The Indian does not demand proof of the otherworld; he realizes it through sacred ritual. The old Dakota warrior at the "Fourth Hill" of his life sings his song to communicate his contact with an invisible world of half magical powers. As for the visible things of samsara (the world. Also the seemingly endless cycle of birth-death-rebirth), "he has utterly herculean conviction that their outer aspects and their inner potencies are wholly incommensurate. The world of sense is a world of shape, shiftings and illusion, behind which move the inevitable forces of the Great Mystery."2. The Western mind looks for meaning in the visible; the Native American, "beyond the visible." The connotations differ in that the West predicates it – the "real world" on "planning, manipulation, predictability, competition, and power, while the other is based on reciprocation, 'flowering' response to situation and cooperation – and who would be surprised to find that the actual symbols and meanings of the two religious modes will be perceived and expressed in quite contrastive forms?"3.

Vedanta and Ramakrishna stress that the main hold maya has over humankind is lust and greed, bondage and future journeys of pleasure and pain, the basis of all desire. People seeking Mukti or liberation from future samsaras must give up these two pleasures of which maya is predicated. Says Ramakrishna, lust is the root of all desires: the root of the tree is lust and the branches and leaves are the desires.

The Sioux would agree with Ramakrishna. In their cosmology there is a god, Iktomi, the spider trickster, capable of many marvelous antics, and he has the ability to change appearances. Iktomi's main task is to assist part of creation: plants, animal or humans bound by maya look foolish. But Iktomi is usually the victim of his own efforts to trap others in his snares.

Joseph Rockboy, an elder of the Yankton Sioux, tells Mark St. Pierre and Tilda Long Soldier a humorous story about the fallible Iktomi: There was a time when Iktomi was walking along the river bank. Iktomi was ready to eat a dinner of prairie chickens he had captured and killed with his cunning. Around the time he was ready to stop and eat, he heard a strange sound – a soft moaning like that of a beautiful woman. In fact, Iktomi was very vain and thought the woman was calling his name, so he strained to hear better, but he could not make out the words. Soon Iktomi's curiosity got the better of him, and he strained his eyes to see if he could spot the woman. Because she was a human woman he figured he'd better make himself resemble a man, so he did.

Soon across the rushing river he thought he saw the woman. The spider imagined she was naked and swayed gently as she moaned. Now, Iktomi thought perhaps she is bathing, and if she sees me she might be frightened. So he decided on a plan to have her.

Iktomi commanded his male part to grow very long and to stretch across the river all the way to the woman. Just as it was about to do so, a coyote came along. "What are you doing, Ikto?" the coyote asked, secretly eyeing the sack full of prairie chicken.

"Why, there is a beautiful woman across the river," he answered, "it is rushing very hard, and I'm not much of a swimmer, and I can't reach her even though very likely she is in love with me." With that Iktomi extended himself, striking the woman where he intended. When he pushed he was stuck tight. As it turned out the beautiful woman was only two twisted cottonwoods, the moaning simply the wind rubbing the trees together. Iktomi pulled and screamed, but could not get free. The coyote laughed at his unfortunate friend, picked up the sack of chicken, and moved off a short distance to eat in peace. By the time Iktomi pulled free, his dinner had been eaten! We shall see that Iktomi was not only a trickster, he wore other hats.

Besides being bound by lust and gold, much of humankind makes God play second fiddle to his most cherished sense-objects. Ramakrishna believes that most people will automatically say, it is God's will when he or she hears of a far-off natural disaster like a hurricane or a train wreck where many people are killed. But when it comes to the death of a loved one or the loss of a personal fortune, it is no longer "God's will." This, too, is maya, says the sage of Dakshineswar.

The Sacred Fools

The Lakota word for the clown is Heyoka. Nick Black Elk called them the "Sacred Fools." Standing Bear referred to them as the "Thunder Dreamers."

Sacred Fools or not, the clown throws the delusions of maya back into his people's faces – sometimes they laugh, sometimes they cry: the clown purposely provokes his audience with shocking antics, he violates all norms, and at the bottom line, his crazy acts are to cause people to laugh, releasing worries lodged in their stomachs, which it is claimed lead to illnesses in general.

Nick Black Elk explains how the Lakota rely on the clown. "Clowns make people observe and think about things in new ways. By causing people to laugh, they clear worry from people's minds and permit them to see higher truths. They teach by 'bad' example. They mock the order of the ritual players' song, holy beings and sacred objects. They joke, satirize and behave contrarily. They do things that are forbidden and unspeakable within ritual framework. They create imbalance and disorder in the world in the midst of rationalized social order. Without the clown's disorders, order would not be so obvious and so justified. Clowns are also believed to cure illnesses." 1. Black Elk also declares that the clown has a positive effect on people's moods, making them "feel jolly" and happy at first so that it may be easier for power to come to them. Comments Black Elk, "In the Heyoka ceremony, everything is backwards, and it is planned that the people shall be made to feel jolly and happy first, so that it may be easier for the power to come to them. You have noticed that the truth comes into this world with two faces. One is sad with suffering, and the other laughs, but it is the same face, laughing or weeping. When people are already in despair, maybe the laughing face is better for them; and when they feel too good and are too sure of being safe, maybe the weeping face is better for them to see. And so I think that is what the Heyoka ceremony is for."2. Vedanta says that tears and laughter are not two separate things, but are inseparable, as in maya, mired in contradiction, all the pairs of opposites are linked together as in life and death, night and day, hot and cold ect., you can't have one without the other; nothing in the world is different in kind only in degree, as Swamiji states the difference between the Nazarene and a worm is not in kind but only in degree.

Lame Deer describes the clown, "as an upside-down, backward-forward, yes and no man."3.Lame Deer also observed that "A sacred clown brings honor, but also shame. It gives you power but you have to pay for it."4.

A Thunder dreamer is said to bring changes in the weather. A person dreaming of thunder or lightning or any symbols of the two has to spend part of his life in an unnatural manner

(See Chapter 20). If a Heyoka haga performs properly power is bestowed upon him to make the rain fall and the wind blow.

Ramakrishna was no stuffed shirt preacher, he could play the clown even when he was in samadhi. "One day he [Habadhari] saw me in an ecstatic mood sitting naked on a branch of the banyan tree in the Panchavati and passing water like a boy. From that day on he was thoroughly convinced that I had been possessed by a ghost."5.

Reincarnation

In the Western religious sense life and death are linear and separated. Because of the belief in only a single lifetime, the Judeo-Christian has an attitude reflected in the old axiom: don't put off until tomorrow what you can do today. The believer in reincarnation takes a less here and now attitude; he or she holds the converse to be the truth – tomorrow is another day. In other words there is an endless round of physical existence (samsara) if one so desires. The Vedantin says an individual returns to this world as a result of his or her karma – good as well as bad – every experience is a teacher for the man or woman on the evolutionary ladder to perfection, or the attainment to the knowledge of the Atman or the higher self. Moreover since an individual is unable to achieve all his or her desires in a single bout with life, he or she is given countless chances for fulfillment. Good or selfless actions make it easier to succeed; bad actions make it harder. Some people even desire intense suffering; in fact, according to some sages, suffering is the hardest thing to renounce.

The Vedantin says the goal of all religion is freedom from the interminable cycle of the pairs of opposites, suffering as well as pleasure. According to Vivekananda, there is a purpose in transmigrating from one physical body to another: to become perfect. "This way it will go on until it has finished its experience and completed the circle. It then vanishes, its powers become manifest, it becomes perfect; no more is there any necessity for it to work through finer or mental bodies. It shines in its own light, and is free; no more to be born, no more to die."1. Vivekananda did not mean to imply that the individual had to be perfect in order to reach God, only as a jivanmukta, or liberated while still in the body – the fate of very few – a saint. One has only to desire it, but desire it intensely, for as Ramakrishna said, "God is a wish fulfilling tree." The theory is that intense spiritual practice (sadhana) will eventually increase one's desire and the individual's desire for worldly pleasures will decrease.

There is no animal body for reborn individuals or jivas, one of the great fallacies of many people outside the Hindu and Buddhist pale. As tough as Ramakrishna is compared to the "grace" of the Holy Mother, the reborn individual does not assume an animal form as the benighted stereotype about the theory of transmigration suggests, but he or she comes back at the same degree of spirituality attained in their previous birth. Nothing is lost, no heaven or hell even for the backslider who turns toward more worldly pursuits. Says Ramakrishna, "If a man slips from the path of yoga, then he is reborn in a prosperous family and starts again his spiritual practices for the realization of God."2.

Many Lakota believe that one may be born more than once, and there are some who claim to have had full knowledge of a former life. There are also those who held converse with a "twin spirit", who have been born into another tribe or race.

"There was a well-known Sioux war-prophet who lived in the middle of the last century," says Ohiyesa, "so that he is still remembered by the old men of his band. After he had reached middle age, he declared that he had a spirit brother among the Ojibways, the ancestral enemies of the Sioux. He even named the band to which his brother belonged, and said that he also was a war-prophet among his people.

"Upon one of their hunts along the border between the two tribes, the Sioux leader one evening called his warriors together, and solemnly declared to them that they were about to meet a like band of Ojibway hunters led by his spirit twin. Since this was to be their first meeting since they were born as strangers; he earnestly begged the young men to resist the temptation to join battle with their tribal foes."3.

The upshot occurred when the prophet suggested to his warriors that his spirit twin would resemble him in every way. Scouts approached the Ojibway camp with a peace pipe. Upon reaching the camp the scouts were crestfallen by the resemblance of the two men who immediately embraced one another. A feast was prepared at the Ojibway camp, and the prophet asked his twin brother to sing one of his sacred songs, which he did to the amazement of the audience, because it was the same song frequently sang by the prophet.

At the Pine Ridge reservation in South Dakota, twins, according to Standing Bear, were people, it was believed, who previously had lived with the tribe some time in the past and had returned to resume their lives among the Lakota. Standing Bear observed twins with ear holes for earrings, which led to the credibility that they had once resided among his people. The spirits of the little twins hovered among the tepees, lifting and poking at the doorways, as they sought a suitable place to be born. Tribal psychics saw and conversed with them, but they disappeared when ordinary people were called forth to observe them.

Twin children were characteristically different than ordinary children. Twin siblings were the closest of companions; they conversed in whispers unheard by ordinary people and were able to flaunt tribal customs and social laws without any consequences. When one twin died the other soon followed.

Lame Deer expands on the topic of twins. "I am always hoping that there will be some twins in the marriages which I perform...You see, love is something that you can't leave behind you when you die. It's that powerful. The Nagi, the soul, it will roam and travel. If two people loved each other very much they come back again as twins. They had a great love, they're whirling around there, and the Great Spirit has pity and lets them come up again. Those little traveling souls come right back in again – twins, triplets, not only lovers but a brother and sister too who were especially fond of each other could come back like this. One reborn this way could carry a memory going way back. I used to know one, a man named, Somebody, who remembered part of his former life over 200 years ago."4.

Dreams in which returned spirits manifest among the living generally fall into two groups among the Lakota. The First pertains to spirits that have returned to assist the living, and become, perhaps at birth, an ally for life. Many spirits used in healing are actually ancestral spirits intended to serve as intermediaries between the incarnate world and the disincarnate world. Part of the Lakota belief in reincarnation is based on the idea that some of those currently alive may be sent back to live again or to help people. Mark St. Pierre and Tilda Long Soldier reveal a story told by an anonymous Lakota woman. "There was a girl in our community who was born with strange scars on her hands that resembled burns. She told people who asked about them, 'I am an old woman who has returned. I was badly burned in my prior life.'"5.

Like the Buddha, many Native Americans believe that humankind is involved in the circle of necessity and thus, is to the wheel of life and death; they deduce that the living do come from the dead and the dead from the living. According to Evans-Wentz, before the coming of the white man and the advent of Christianity, the American Indian was stoic about the inevitability of the cessation of his body. He composed a death song and "religiously was like a hero going home." "In former days, before being corrupted by the white man, every Indian brave committed to memory a Death Song, often of his own composing, for use when he knew that the inevitable end had come. He sang the Death Song, as did the famous Apache Medicine-man and war chief, Geronimo (circa 1834-1909), and died not with fear and trembling, as many white men do, but heroically like a hero going home. From youth he was trained to be prepared to meet death, as the Oriental yogin is, with the assurance of having made the best use of opportunities afforded by human birth."6.

Life and death are inseparably intertwined in the Dakota lore. In the ritual of the Fourth Hill, the elderly warrior has traversed the meaning of joy and sorrow, the plane of contradiction or maya and, thus, he is more conversant with the spiritual meanings of death.

There is a Blackfoot Sioux myth of tribal Grandsire and Grandmother, who debate the question of eternal life or immortality. "In the beginning Old Man and Old Woman debated whether people should die. 'People will never die,' said Old Man. 'Oh,' said Old Woman, 'that will never do… if people live always there will be too many people in the world.' 'Well,' said Old Man, 'we do not want to die forever. We shall die for four days, and then come to life again.' 'Oh no!' said Old Woman, 'it will be better to die forever, so that we shall be sorry for each other.'"7. According to figures on the Internet, 27 million Americans believe in reincarnation.

The Seven Campfires of the Sioux: The Circle

Says Lame Deer, "Circles within a larger circle, part of the larger hoop which [is] the seven campfires of the Sioux, represents one nation."1.

The circular view of the universe and the world strongly adhered to by the Oglala Sioux, summarizes a religious point of view held by many Native Americans. The Lakota believe that practically all aspects of nature operate under the laws of cycles. On the more observable level this certainly includes every empirical form of life. According to Nick Black Elk, "Everything the power of the world does is done in a circle. The sky is round, and I have heard that the earth is round like a ball, and so are all stars. The wind in its greatest power whirls. Birds make their nests in circles, for their's is the same religion as ours. The sun comes forth and goes down in a circle. The moon does the same, and both are round. Even the seasons form a great circle in their changing, and always come back again to where they were. The life of man is a circle from childhood to childhood, and so it is in everything where power moves. Our tepees were round like the nests of birds, and these were always set in a circle, the nations' hoop, a nest of many nests, where the Great Spirit meant for us to hatch our children."2.

Swami Vivekananda expands on this concept. "Next we learn that all these particular forms, whether they are plants, animals, or men, are being repeated ad infinitum, rising and falling. The seed produces the tree, the tree produces the seed, which again comes up as another tree. And so on and on. There is no end to it. Water drops roll down the mountains into the ocean, and rise again as vapor, going back to the mountains, and again coming down to the ocean. So rising and falling, the cycle goes on."3.

The Oglala perceive the harmony in the interminable circle of creation and recreation. When they die their bodies are interred, returning nourishment to the earth, in turn the earth makes plants grow; the plants feed the animals, the animals feed humanity. Comments Lame Deer, "Nothing is so small and unimportant but it has a spirit given to it by Wakan-Tanka. Tunkan is what you might call a stone god, but he is also part of the Great Spirit. The gods are separate beings, but they are all united in Wakan-Tanka. It is hard to understand – something like the Holy Trinity. You can't explain it except by going back to the 'circles within circles' idea, the spirit splitting itself into stones, trees, tiny insects even making them all Wakan by his ever-presence. And in turn all these myriad of things which makes up the universe flowing back to their source, united in the one Grandfather spirit." All aspects of God, "Tunkcan, the stone spirit, Wakinyan, the thunder spirit, Takuskanska, the moving spirit, Unktehi, the water spirit – they are all Wakan – mysterious, wonderful, incomprehensible, holy. They are all part of the Great Mystery."4.

Swamiji suggests that there is a relationship between a circle and the soul. "There is no motion in a straight line. Everything moves in a circle. A straight line infinitely produced, becomes a circle. If that is the case, there cannot be eternal degeneration of any soul. It cannot be. Everything must complete the circle and come back to its source."5. Vivekananda speaks of the power of gravity and the circle. If a person throws a stone into the air with enough velocity and waits long enough, the stone will return to the palm of his outstretched hand.

The late Mexican Nobel Laureate, Octavio Paz, sees the cyclical pattern in Mexican sculpture. "Matter and meaning are fused together: the stone speaks and becomes an idea; and the idea is transformed into stone."6.

The Other Side Camp

Most religions foresee the continued existence of the individual soul in a world very much like our own, only there is happiness, and no misery. There is much hanky panky as the senses are allowed free reign – wine, woman and song. The Muslims have rivers of wine and houri girls. A similar fare is forecast in other creeds. Only in Judeo-Christianity is it a little bit vaguer, but promises the believer an eternal companionship with Christ. But for the wrongdoer and the heretic an eternal eternity in hell or maybe purgatory. Vedanta calls these livable places Swargas, admitting the unblemished pleasures, but contradicting the word "eternal" with the killjoy declaration that these realms, including hell, are only temporary since they, too, are under the jurisdiction of maya; so the meritorious individual has to return to this world to resume his or her struggle for the realization of God. Vivekananda says, "Thank God for giving you this world as a moral gymnasium." Deceased individuals receiving these dividends have had to perform a few meritorious deeds – building hospitals or roads, bestowing funds for charities and orphanages with the idea of going to heaven. There are vast numbers of jivas or deceased people in these heavens, having indestructible, beautiful bodies with the clock ticking away. Vivekananda describes it this way, "The only so-called higher beings are the departed, and these are nothing but men who have taken another body. This is finer, it is true, but still a man-body, with hands and feet, and so on. And they live on this earth in another Akasa, without being absolutely invisible. They also think, and have consciousness and everything else like us. So they also are men, so are the Devas [gods], the angels. But man alone becomes God; and they all have to become men again in order to become God."1.

One Lakota version is the "Other side Camp", which has Christian overtones with a Siouan flavor. The soul journeys until it sees a tipi inhabited by an old man (Wakan-Tanka), who queries it about its merits and demerits on its journey through life. A favorable judgment merits it a permanent habitation in the "Happy Mirror", a sphere or similar to the Camelot mentioned by Standing Bear. An unfavorable judgment lands the sojourner back on earth "to learn more." Or to the Land of Many Lodges, not dissimilar to the paradigm of most religions. "The Land of many lodges was a fabulous place. Here were pitched the tipis of all one's ancestors. Here were one's friends and relatives living amidst lush park-lands rich in the good things of nature. Buffalo and other animals roamed the land in unending abundance. This was a good land, a land where all things which had ever existed now lived for eternity." 2.The Rig Veda Samhita

(The most ancient records of Aryan India) would agree with the concept thoroughly.

On the other hand, Ohiyesa says that this land of Many Lodges or "happy hunting ground" was a fabrication of the white man, rather, "The Indian never doubted the immortal nature of the spirit or soul of man, but neither did he care to speculate upon its probable state or condition in a future life. The idea of a 'happy hunting ground' is modern and probably borrowed or invented by the white man. The primitive Indian was content to believe that the spirit which the 'Great Mystery' breathed into man returns to Him who gave it, and that after it is freed from the body, it is everywhere and pervades all nature, yet often lingers near the grave or 'spirit bundle' for the consolation of friends, and is able to hear prayers. So much reverence was due the disembodied spirit that it was not customary with us even to name the dead aloud."3.

Another Lakota view is a scenario most psychics could be comfortable with – a parallel world where the embodied and disembodied can interact through the mediations of a medium.

Severt Young Bear, an Oglala, gives his "steps on the Red Road." He lays out seven steps a person must take through his or her life from a toddler to old age called "loneliness." It is not too distant from the nonsecular Western idea except for the posthumous experience of a future life on earth. If the "soul" dies incomplete, i.e., dies too soon or fails unsuccessfully on one of Young Bear's seven paths, "then it will be sent back to live on this earth again until it completes the journey 'in a good way.'"4.

Madonna Swan, a Lakota woman gives her account of a remarkable near-death or out-of-body experience. Much of her version is close to the universal, near-death themes of Raymond Moody and others who wrote widely on the subject. In Madonna Swan's semi comatose state in a Bismarck, North Dakota hospital, she is reacquainted with Levi, a childhood sweetheart killed in an accident while Madonna was undergoing treatment for tuberculosis.

In an altered state of mind Madonna finds herself enclosed in a dreary long-log hall with former members of her family, all deceased. Suddenly the spirits become animated and begin to dance, whereby Madonna is interrupted by an anonymous man, who announces the arrival of a visitor, waiting for her outside the door. Madonna relates her strange encounter with Levi, her first love. "I left the circle and started walking towards the door. I got to the door, opened it, and here was Levi! And Gee! The hills were green, and covered with flowers all over the ground! There was every kind of tree, and it was pretty there. Prettier than any place I had ever been. There were birds of every kind, and they were singing. The colors were so beautiful."5.

Levi beckons Madonna and tells her to follow him, but every time she draws nearer, he moves farther way.

Levi asks her to join him at the edge of a beautiful blue stream, and although she hesitates, she reveals her ambivalence about following him. "Well, I thought, if it's that important to him, I'll go down there. When I got down there, I thought to myself, you know, this man is dead, and I'm talking to him. Now he's trying to get me through that water, or I'll die. So I just stood there and Levi started through the water. He was up to his knees in the water, then his waist. 'Come and wade in the water with me, it's not cold,' he said. 'It's really warm. These rocks won't hurt your feet.' 'But,' I said, 'Oh, I can't wade in the water with my bare feet. I'm just going to leave my shoes on.'"6.

Madonna enters the stream cautiously until the water

reaches her knees. But Levi, the water chest-high, announces he has something to tell her. The youngsters never actually make contact, because Madonna in a frightful state of mind leaves the water and backtracks toward the lodge, Levi in tow. Suddenly, as her breathing becomes impaired, a nurse who asks her, "Did you have a dream?" startles her awake? "Yeah," I finally said, "I guess it was a dream." Madonna couldn't explain to the nonplused nurse that, "I think it was in the place where all my dead relatives are. That must be wherever I was." "Saying this before I was awake enough to realize it wasn't making any sense trying to tell this to the nurse."7.

Madonna Swan concludes her near-death experience, "I have never had a dream like that! I believe I must have been close to death. It is a beautiful, wonderful place there. Since that time I haven't been afraid of death. I know what's on the other side. It's a beautiful place, and Levi wants me to join him there."8.

The Lakota's faith in God is so strong that they believe the deity can make the impossible possible. Mel Lone Hill, vice chairman of the Oglala Sioux band (1983) was a patient of medicine woman, Lucille Kills Enemy, a full Lowanpi priest. Lucille entered the spirit world to retrieve Mel Lone Hill whose spirit had passed over to the Otherside Camp. Comments Mel Lone Hill, "She doctored me at our house. Four years in a row I'd had pneumonia, and the last one killed me. I was gone. She had to find me on the other side. She was probably the only one I knew of who was that powerful. I think she was in her mid eighties when she doctored me."9. In some cases the shaman visits the abode of the dead to return the subtle form that had left his or her physical body, but was not completely dead.

When near-death patients return to the world of the living,

the Lakota consider these people Wakan or mysterious. The Lakota are not unique to these phenomena: eight million Americans claim to have had similar experiences.

Vivekananda was disinclined to have provided a lengthy discourse on Brahma Loka, the highest sphere of which there is no return to earth for these liberated spirits. The Swami spoke volumes about the swargas and suggested his devotees pray to avoid going there. Actually in Vedanta philosophy, the departed only apparently enter heaven or hell and this earth, which are all maya, a mere dream. In his beautiful statement describing these experiences as a mere drop in the ocean, he says, "Neither can there be birth or death for the soul. Dying, and being born, reincarnation, and going to heaven, cannot be for the soul. These are different appearances, different mirages, different dreams. If a man who is dreaming of this world now dreams of wicked thoughts and wicked deeds, after a certain time the thought of that very dream will produce the next dream. He will dream that he is in a horrible place, being tortured. The man who is dreaming good thoughts and good deeds, after that period of dream is over, will dream he is in a better place; and so on from dream to dream. But the time will come when the whole of this dream will vanish. To everyone of us there must come a time when the whole universe will be found to have been a mere dream, when we shall find that the soul is infinitely better than its surroundings. In this struggle through what we call our environments, there will come a time when we shall find that these environments were almost zero in comparison with the power of the soul. It is only a question of time, and time is nothing in the Infinite. It is a drop in the ocean. We can afford to wait and be calm."10.

The Holy Mother reveals a little more about the denouement

of liberated souls. As for the devotees of Ramakrishna, she sometimes said, "For you there is the Ramakrishna-loka, the heaven where Sri Ramakrishna is eternally present with his intimate disciples."11. In regards to Ramakrishna Loka [The Holy Mother told a disciple that Ramakrishna was going to create a Ramakrishna Loka for his liberated devotees). The Holy Mother seemed to imply that on this highest plane of existence, "There are two classes of devotees, one devotes itself to the service of God, as on this earth; and another group is immersed in meditation for ages."12.

Many people might fear that in this elevated sphere, they would lose their prized sense of individuality or is- ness and blend into nothingness as their ego is dissolved into zero. Vivekananda explains that individuality itself is but an illusion. "There is no real individuality of the Jiva (separate soul); eventually it as a compound will go to pieces. Only that which is beyond further analysis is 'simple', and that alone is truth, freedom, immortality, bliss. All struggles for the preservation of this illusive individuality are really vices. All struggles to lose this individuality are virtues. Everything in the universe is trying to break down this individuality, either consciously or unconsciously. All morality is based upon the destruction of separateness or false individuality, because that is the cause of all sin."13.

The great consolation of Christianity was the message it preached of bodily resurrection in which the continuance of the human personality or ego was to be reconstituted in heaven. Based on the resurrection of Jesus, Christianity was among the few religions to confront directly the question of total personality survival.

Holy Mother states that even the notion of the gods and such are maya. "In the course of time one does not feel even the existence of God. After attaining wisdom [jnana], one sees that gods and deities are all maya. Everything comes into existence in time and also disappears in time...Deities and such things really disappear at the dawn of knowledge. The aspirant then realizes that the Mother alone pervades the entire universe. All become one. This is the simple truth."14. Again Vivekananda, "Those who receive this knowledge are one with the universe. For them, all heavens and even Brahmaloka are destroyed, the whole dream vanishes, and they find themselves the eternal God of the universe. They attain their real individuality, with its infinite knowledge and bliss, and become free. Pleasures in little things cease. We are finding pleasure in this little body, in this little individuality. How much greater the pleasure when this whole universe is my body! If there is pleasure in one body, how much more when all bodies are mine! Then is freedom attained. And all this is called Advaita, the non-dualistic Vedanta philosophy."15.

Swami explains that a Christ or Buddha seen through maya becomes the personal god or avatar, or as the Bible states, "the word made flesh." "The Personal God is the same absolute looked at through the haze of Maya. When we approach Him with the five senses, we can see Him only as the personal God. The idea is that the Self cannot be objectified. How can the Knower know Itself? But It can cast a shadow as it were, if that can be called objectification. So the highest form of that shadow, that attempt at objectifying Itself, is the Personal God."16.

The Mother of Songs

The Mother of Songs – the mother of our whole seed bore us in the beginning. She is the mother of all races of men and the mother of tribes. She is the mother of the thunder, the mother of the rivers, the mother of trees and mother of songs and dances. She is the mother of the older brother stones. She is the mother of the grain and the mother of all things. She is the mother of the younger brother Frenchmen and the strangers. She is the mother of the dance paraphernalia and all temples, and the only mother we have. She is the mother of the animals, the only one, and the mother of the Milky Way. It was the mother herself who began to baptize. She gave us the limestone coca dish. She is the mother of the rain, the only one we have. She alone is the mother of things, she alone. And the mother has left a memory in all temples. With her sons, the saviors, she left songs and dances as a reminder. Thus the priests, the fathers have reported. (Song of the Kagaba Indians of Columbia).

Most of us live in the realm of things and multiplicity, and it is difficult, indeed, to conceive of a world, a universe without name and form, or of living things without attaching a gender to them. Abstractions like the absolute must of necessity be susceptible to the inclinations of the human mind. Ramakrishna stated many times, "When a thorn [ignorance] runs into the body, one has to take it out by means of another [knowledge] and then throw both away."

Lame Deer humorously recounts his stereotype of the Great Spirit – like an Old Testament prophet with a beard – being conked on the head by the unexpected wisdom of a medicine man. "Tell me about the Great Spirit," I asked him [a medicine man]. "He is not like a human being, like a white god. He is a power. That power could be in a cup of coffee. The Great Spirit is no old man with a beard."1.

One of the fundamental principles shared by Eastern mystics and Native America is the concept of Mother worship. The gynocentric universe springs from the idea that the feminine part of the male-female dyad has not only an equal role in the play of creation but a superior one. From the creative cycle of the kalpa, the Great Mystery, and Genesis culminate into forms of Mother worship still prevalent in India and on the soil of indigenous America. Thus, it is not surprising that Ramakrishna worshiped the Divine Mother as his Ishadevata or Chosen Ideal.

In terms of the gender dichotomy, the entire universe and all its multiplicity is divided into two poles or pairs of opposites, and is permeated by a secret energy or power emanating from the single source of all being – Brahman/ the Great Spirit. The gynocentric view is that the dynamic force in humanity and the universe is female – the Hindu

Shakti, and the passive pole – the Hindu male Shiva. The subordinate masculine principle creates the cosmos by exercising its power to produce change. The gynocentric devotee meditates on Shakti as energy, and on Shiva as quiescent wisdom. "Brahman and Shakti are identical," says Ramakrishna, "like fire and its power to burn. Again the fire's power to burn implies the fire itself. If you accept the one you must accept the other."2.

Wallace Black Elk agrees, "All the shapes and forms of life originate from the fire. In your scientific language you call it the atom. The rock we call Maka. Maka is the Earth. So we have Grandfather who is the wisdom, and Grandmother who is the knowledge. But the wisdom and knowledge are really one."3.

The symbolic representing the feminine aspect of the universe have blended with Vedic thought to encompass the idea that woman is the arcanum of being and becoming. The whole creation and the process of becoming represent the explosion of the primordial unity and the division of the two primary principles – Shiva and Shakti; both elements are necessary for the process. It is Prakriti (feminine principle) that labors, engenders, and nourishes. The gods call upon Shakti when the universe is endangered.

Ramakrishna describes his Divine Mother's role in the creation cycle of the universe. "After the destruction of the universe, my Divine Mother, the embodiment of Brahman, gathers together the seeds for the next creation. After the creation the Primal Power dwells in the universe itself. She brings forth this phenomenal world and then pervades it. In the Vedas creation is likened to the spider and its web. The spider brings the web out of itself and then remains in it. God is the container of the universe and also what is contained in it."4.

"The practitioners of Mother worship among the Sioux function by thought, using language, movement, sound, painting, drawing, mimetics, gestures, dress, laughter, shock, herbs, minerals, and repetitive devices as foci for that thought. Most of all they use their ability to deal adeptly in supernatural realms to achieve their objective, depending on long training, familiarity with Great Mysteries and its (their) ways and contacts among supernaturals. The ability to dance, drum, chant dramatically or alter consciousness so that one can see amazing things are of little use without the aid and protection of some helpers from the other side."5.

The Good Red Road:
The White Buffalo Calf Woman

I am a woman
I hold up half the sky
I am a woman
I nourish half the earth.
I am a woman
I nourish half the earth.
The rainbow touches my shoulders.
*The universe encircles my eyes.*1.

The Good Red Road – North – South is to the Lakota the path of life. The feminine Shakti aspect of Brahman or the Great Spirit is also the personal God; she appears among many kinds of people of differing cultures and races: she appeared in human form among the Jewish people as the Virgin Mary, the mother of Jesus. It was said she was clothed with the sun. She appeared to the acolyte boy, Juan Diego, with an Indian visage and called herself the Virgin of Guadalupe. She appeared to the French teenager, Bernadette Soubirous, at Lourdes and called herself the Immaculate Conception, and so, the Word made Flesh.

"The Sioux chose for their tutelary deity a woman, rather than a man, indicates their concern to revere feminine qualities. That the Buffalo Maiden was in fact, the Goddess Whope, wife of Okaga, the South Wind, enforced the proposition that the Sioux savior was completely and wholesomely feminine. She firmly established a rigid yet healthy, realistic sexual pattern to which both its men and its women could subscribe, and which they could respect."2.

The White Buffalo (Calf) Woman or Maiden brought her people a code of behavior. Instead of the paternal rigidity of "Thou Shall Not- " her commands were always phrased gently in the positive, "Be kind to woman and children." The Sioux embraced this maternal set of new values, indispensable in sustaining them from the destructive forces always imminent at their doorstep. The White Buffalo Woman manifested among the Sioux at a troublesome time (1780, according to Mark St. Pierre and Tilda Long Soldier) when the bands were forced out of the lush forests and food-providing lakes of Minnesota and Wisconsin on to the harsh plains where endurance was difficult. In the Lakota lexicon she is called Ptehincalasanwin or just "Holy Woman."

No less than that of the White Buffalo Woman, is the beautiful Buddhist Bodhisattva, Kuan Yin, who always endeavored to cast out all fear and to have fulfilled all longings. Kuan Yin's method of handling small-minded meanness was her display of stern disapproval, and she lovingly punished solely to teach those she chastised.

Lame Deer says that the Lakota see Jesus and Wakan Tanka

as the same; so are God and the White Buffalo Woman. Christ and the stone in the medicine bottle, the light from the kerosene lamp and the Holy Spirit: "the Holy Spirit is like a sharp-eyed eagle. You can't fool him."

But there is a side to the feminine Shakti in her role of destroyer: she creates, sustains and destroys. The black image of Mother Kali is venerated throughout Hindu India. Sometimes known as the Divine Mother, Ramakrishna clarifies this multifaceted power of Syama-Kali and her contradictory aspects. "Syama-Kali has a somewhat tender aspect and is worshipped in the Hindu households. She is the Dispenser of boons and the Dispeller of fear. People worship Raksha-Kali, the Protectress in times of epidemic, famine, earthquake, drought and flood. Smasana-Kali is the embodiment of the power of destruction. She resides in the cremation ground, surrounded by corpses, jackals, and terrible female spirits. From Her mouth flows a stream of blood, from Her neck hangs a garland of human heads, and around Her waist is a girdle made of human heads."3.

Swamiji said Kali is not for Western Vedantists. In a letter to Mary Hale, a well-known devotee, he noted, "Kali worship is not a necessary step in any religion. The Upanishads teach us all there is of religion. Kali worship is my special fad, you never heard me preach it, or read of my preaching it in India. I only preach what is good for universal humanity. If there is any curious method which applies entirely to me, I keep it a secret and there it ends. I must not explain to you what Kali-worship is, as I never taught it to anybody."4.

The White Buffalo Woman's story is foremost concerned with the Sacred Pipe, the primary icon of the Sioux nation. There are many versions of this story, and Lame Deer's rendition is among the clearest and right to the point.

"Our grandfathers told us how the sacred pipe was brought

to our tribes. One summer, untold lifetimes ago, our different bands gathered for their yearly get-together. The earth was beautiful, covered with high grass and flowers, but the people were hungry...Among the Sioux, the Itazipcho – the 'Without Bows' tribe – had not had any meat for days. They decided to send out two hunters to scout for buffalo.

"The two men searched a long time for game without finding any. At last they came to the top of a hill from which they had a good view, and they saw something moving toward them. At first they thought it was a buffalo, but as it came nearer it turned out to be a beautiful young woman, the most beautiful they had ever seen. She wore a finely made dress of white buckskin so wonderfully decorated that no human hands could have made it. She wore a bundle on her back and carried a fan of sage leaves in her hand."5.

Lame Deer said her name was White Buffalo Woman. Then the goddess addressed the two hunters. "Do not be afraid. I have come from the buffalo nation with a message for your people, a good message."6. So lovely was Buffalo Woman that one of the hunters became overcome with lust and tried to possess her. But she was Lila Wakan, a goddess, and the story goes on to say that as soon as the hunter attempted to seize her, a cloud descended and encapsulated him, and he turned into a pile of dry bones as his punishment. But this denouement was only speculative, according to Lame Deer, it was the man's desire which destroyed him, as such desire has brought ruination to many before and after him.

In the mythical Hindu tale from the Chandi, the Devi Mahatmyam is much like the White Buffalo Woman. The goddess, Mahatmyam takes the form of a very beautiful woman who tempts the lusts of the power-crazed deities or demons, the Asuras, who hasten to possess her, only to be destroyed when she manifests her destructive power.

By now only a single hunter remained in the party. White Buffalo Woman told him to return to his people to prepare them for her arrival. White Buffalo Woman explained what she wanted them to do: to erect a large tipi and to make a sacred earth altar called Owanka Wakan inside. White Buffalo Woman further wanted the Sioux to place a buffalo skull and a rack composed of three sticks inside the tipi. The buffalo skull or any other part of the animal contains the power of the buffalo.

In the course of a short duration, everything was accomplished exactly as White Buffalo Woman specified, after the hunter returned to his people and told them that a sacred woman was coming among them the following morning with a message from the Buffalo Nation.

As the sun rose the next morning, the Sioux assembled around the sacred tipi and, "They saw the White Buffalo Woman coming toward them in a sacred manner. Instead of the sage fan she carried the holy pipe. She was holding the stem with her right hand and the bowl with her left, and that is how we carry the pipe to this day."7.

When the goddess entered the tipi, the hapless Indians told her of their undernourished plight. "Sister, we are glad that you came. We have had no meat for some time and all we can offer you is water."8.

And according to Nick Black Elk in another account, White Buffalo Woman sang:

With visible Breath
I am walking
A voice I am sending as I walk
In a sacred manner I am walking.
With visible tracks I am walking.
*In a sacred manner I walk.*9.

The hunters dipped some sweet grass called Wacanga into a skin bag filled with water and gave it to White Buffalo Woman, "And to this day we dip sweetgrass or an eagle feather into water and sprinkle it on those we wish to cure or purify during a ceremony," says Lame Deer, "most of our rites end with the drinking of water, and all this constantly reminds us of the White Buffalo Woman."10.

"The Maiden is said to have come to earth among men over ten generations ago. At this time, the Sioux were engaged in a losing struggle with the powerful Chippewa, a struggle which gave every indication of unequivocal defeat. Supernatural aid took the form not of a secret and powerful weapon or a political trump, but of an effective code and symbol of peace – the pipe."11.

White Buffalo Woman showed the Indians how to use the pipe. She filled it with red willow bark tobacco. Then she walked in a sacred manner representing the symbolic circle without end, the road of humans from youth to old age, from ignorance to knowledge. White Buffalo Woman walked sunrise or clockwise around the altar. She lit the pipe with a dry buffalo chip that was heated on the fire.

The next step was to show the Sioux how to pray with the pipe by lifting it skyward (hupa gluza) and lowering it toward the earth, pointing it in all four sacred directions. "With this holy pipe you will walk like a living prayer," she told the people, "your feet resting upon the grandmother, the pipe stem reaching all the way up into the sky to the grandfather, your body linking the Sacred Beneath with the Sacred Above. Wakan Tanka smiles on us, because now we are one, earth, sky, all living things and the ikce wicasa – the human beings. Now we are one big family. This pipe binds us together. It is a peacemaker. There is a pool of blood somewhere, a place you came from. You will find this blood petrified into stone and it is red. It comes from a sacred spot common to all people, where even enemies are turned into friends and relatives."12. Lame Deer further explains, "The Omaha tribe had a legend about the pipestone quarry (a sacred spot White Buffalo Woman was referring to). They say that long ago there was an Omaha woman called Wakegela. She was married to a Sioux warrior. One day she found herself face to face with a white buffalo. She followed this sacred animal as if in a trance. She watched the buffalo kicking loose large chunks of red stone and knew right away that these were petrified bodies of her forebears. In this way she discovered the quarry. The Sioux and the Omahas were enemies, but they agreed that they would never fight each other at this sacred place. The land belonged to the Sioux, but the stone belonged to all Indians who honored the pipe."13.

White Buffalo Woman then took up the status of the women, praising their tribal role as workers and mothers. It was the work of their hands and the fruit of their wombs that preserved the tribe. "You are from the mother earth," she told them. "The task which has been given you is as great as the one given to the warrior and hunter."14.

Leonard Crow Dog describes a ceremony, "That is done when a girl reaches womanhood. It is called Wakayapi, meaning 'throwing the ball.' It also is one of the seven sacred rites [that the White Buffalo Woman taught the Sioux] and likewise it is a buffalo ceremony. We have a legend of how it started. Long ago a man had a vision sent to him by Ptesan win. In it he saw a buffalo calf changing itself into a human girl. She had in her hand a ball made of buffalo skin stuffed with buffalo hair, and she threw it up into the air toward a small herd of buffalo and, immediately, these, too, turned themselves into human. The man who received this vision understood that he was to start a new ceremony, and so the

Tapa Wakayapi was born."15.

The sacred pipe became a sacred object, binding both genders in a circle of love, because both sexes participated together in fashioning replicas of the pipe. The men carved out the bowl and manufactured the stem, while the women decorated it with their beautiful quillwork.

White Buffalo Woman's final task was to address the welfare of the children because, according to Lame Deer, they have an understanding beyond their years and, among the Sioux, they have the right to be treated equally with the grownups. White Buffalo Woman acknowledges that the children were the tribe's greatest possession representing the continuity of the people, as represented as a circle without end. "Remember this," she told the children, "grow up and teach your children."

When she was about to take her leave, White Buffalo Woman wrapped the pipe in the bundle she carried on her back and left it for safekeeping with the Old-man chief of the Without Bows: sometimes known as Standing Hollow Horn, and other times known as Buffalo Standing Upward. In addition to the pipe White Woman presented to the Without Bows another gift. It was a round, blood-red stone. It was inscribed with seven circles – the seven campfires of the Lakotas, or the seven ceremonies which go with the pipe. The stone represented the entire universe.

White Buffalo Woman departed in the same direction she had arrived. As she set forth, she sang her song, "Niya Tamiya Mawani ye." Or "With visible breath I am walking." As the people witnessed her departure, the beautiful goddess turned into a white buffalo and disappeared over the horizon. According to Lame Deer, the significance of this has a deeper meaning. "First Niya Tamiya means not only breathing and breath but also being alive and life itself. It means that as long as we honor the pipe we will live, will remain ourselves. And the thought of visible breath can be taken as the smoke of the pipe, which is the breath of our people. It also reminds us of the breath of the buffalo as it can be seen on a cold day. It underlines the fact that for us the pipe and the buffalo are one."16.

In Lame Deer's scheme of things, the pipe given to his ancestors remains to this day as an heirloom. It is called Ptehin-cala Huku canunpa or Buffalo Calf Bone Pipe. Wallace Black Elk preferred the term "Canunpa" and believed it is instrumental in instigating participation with the spirit world. The subsequent pipes used by the Lakota are modeled on the one bequeathed by White Buffalo Woman – made from red pipestone in the way White Buffalo Woman taught the people. Nothing of any significance in the affairs of the tribe can occur without the pipe replica of the original. "If a man killed a tribal brother," Lame Deer asserts, "be it through anger or through accident, then the sacred circle was broken and a wound had been inflicted on the whole people. The killer would see his victim's face reflected in the water every time he drank. When there was a shedding of blood only an untying ceremony with the sacred pipe could bring peace to the minds of the people and reconcile the families involved."17.

The sacred pipe is a holy lie detector among Lame Deer's people. Nobody would be foolish enough to tell a lie while the pipe was passed around, because a lie could prove fatal to a dishonest person.

The pipe played a central role in the religion of the Sioux nation. It was instrumental in bringing about peace with other tribes, and sometimes with traditional enemies: Wolakota wa yaka cola, "Peace without slavery." "There are none to keep them from war except the Pipe of Peace," declares Standing Bear, "if this sacred symbol was taken to Lakota warriors in the thickest battle they would at once obey its mandate and retire."18. "Peace – that ideal which man may sometimes reach – was symbolized in the pipe of peace and under the society of the pipe, or codes symbolized by the pipe, native man made the most effective effort at arriving at peace ever made on this continent. It was but a start, perhaps, but its strength lay in the fact that under the Great Peace, women had begun the necessary foundational work for the elimination of war by raising sons who could participate only in pursuits of peace. War was excluded from the existence of a certain portion of the male population and in this move the Indian mother pointed the way and the only road to the realization of peace between all men. The acceptance of a kinship with other orders of life was the first step toward humanization and the second step was the dedication of sons to peace, the spiritual value of which is incalculable; and not until the women of the land come back to the forsaken road, emulate the Indian mother, and again raise sons for peace will there be any substantial move toward 'peace on earth and good will toward men.'"19.

In 1857 on the Missouri river, the famous Sioux warrior, Sitting Bull, armed with a gun and wearing his Strong Heart bonnet and white blanket coat struck with his lance the Hoke teenager, whom he later saved and adopted as his brother, named Jumping Bull. "Adoptions of captives happened in real life. Around 1857 the Lakota were at war with the Hoke, the Assiniboin. The Lakota came across a small party of Hoke and killed them all, except a young boy about eleven or twelve years old, and they were about to kill him, too. This young boy was brave. He stood his ground and did not cry. He had a little bow, more a toy than a weapon. At this moment Sitting Bull came riding up. He cried, 'This boy is too brave to kill. Don't shoot him! I'll adopt him as my brother!' They took the Hoke boy back to camp and there they had a ceremony in which the Hoke boy became Sitting Bull's Mihunka. His name was Jumping Bull. In every one of Sitting Bull's battles Jumping Bull fought at his side. When many years later, some forty tribal police members surrounded Sitting Bull's one-room log cabin to arrest and kill the great chief, there was a big shootout. When this fight ended, six of the tribal police members and six of Sitting Bull's friends were lying dead on the ground, among them Jumping Bull, who went to the spirit world with his ate hunka. He died like a hunka should, faithful to the end. So, adopting a captive is one of our customs."20.

Lame Deer mentions the seven ceremonies associated with the pipe which White Buffalo Woman offered the Sioux as part of the journey along the Good Red Road. The most reverent to the Oglala and to other members of the Sioux family, as well as many tribes inhabiting the Great Plains was and is the much noted Sun Dance. It was as much a solemn occasion as a festive one.

Nick Black Elk supplies an interesting narrative to go with this occasion. "About the middle of the Moon Making Fat (June) the whole village moved a little way up the River to a good place for a sun dance…Scouts were sent out in all directions to guard the sacred place. Sitting Bull, who was the greatest medicine man of the nation at that time, had charge of this dance to purify the people and to give them power and endurance. It was held in the Moon of Fatness because that is when the sun is highest and the growing power of the world is the strongest. I will tell you how it was done. First a holy man was sent out all alone to find the Waga Chun [cottonwood tree], the holy tree that should stand in the middle of the dancing circle: Nobody dared follow to see what he did or hear the sacred words he would say there. And when he had found the right tree, he would tell the people, and they would come there singing, with flowers all over them. Then when they had gathered about the holy tree, some women who were bearing children would dance around it, because the Spirit of the Sun loves all fruitfulness. After that a warrior, who had done some very brave deed that summer, struck the tree...and when he had done this, he had to give gifts to those who had least of everything, and the braver he was, the more he gave away.

"After this, a band of young maidens came singing, with sharp axes in their hands; and they had to be so good that nobody there could say anything against them, or that any man had ever known them; and it was the duty of any one who knew anything bad about any of them to tell it right before all the people there and prove it. But if anybody lied, it was very bad for him.

"The maidens chopped the tree down and trimmed its branches off. Then chiefs, who were the sons of chiefs, carried the sacred tree home, stopping four times on the way, once for each season, giving thanks for each.

"Now when the holy tree had been brought home but was not yet set up in the center of the dancing place, mounted warriors gathered around the circle of the village, and at a signal they all charged inward upon the center where the tree would stand, each trying to be the first to touch the sacred place; and whoever was the first could not be killed in war that year. When they all came together in the middle, it was like a battle, with the ponies rearing and screaming in a big dust and the men shouting and wrestling and trying to throw each other off the horses.

After that there was a big feast and plenty for everybody to eat, and a big dance just as though we had won a victory."21.

Swami Vivekananda believes the Mother is important to all religions because, "All-merciful, all-powerful, omnipresent are attributes of Divine Mother. She is the sum total of the energy in the universe. Every manifestation of power in the universe is 'Mother.' She is life, She is intelligence, She is love...She can show Herself to us in any form at any moment. Divine Mother can have form (Rupa) and name (Nama) or name without form; and as we worship Her in these various aspects we can rise to Pure Being, having neither form nor name."22.

The Cosmo Theistic Gestalt

Contrary to popular misconception among the non-Indian community, the Native American does not hold to the notion of lycanthropy – the human being takes the form of an animal or has it as his double, nor does he or she believe that the human soul transmigrates into animal bodies. The animals displayed on Indian totems or emblazoned on their shields or other artifacts are but so many symbols of stages in which humankind had to evolve to reach the highest stage of evolution – the human being. This compares positively with the Eastern metaphysics of the souls transmigration of many births moving up the evolutionary rungs until it reaches human birth – the highest stage. It is Brahman or the Great Spirit at play in innumerable forms with experiences sui generis to a particular physical form.

Vivekananda found that of all things of this universe from the smallest atom or particle to the highest god man, have the same soul (atman) even animals. "People in this country think it horrible that humans should evolve from animals. Why? What will be the outcome of these millions of animals? Are they nothing? If we have a soul, so do they, and if they don't neither do we. It's absurd to say that humans alone have a soul and animals have none. I've seen people worse than animals. The soul has sojourned in lower and higher forms, migrating from one to another, according to its samskaras or impressions. But it's only in the highest forms as humans that it attains freedom. Humans are even higher than angels. Of all forms humans are the highest in creation, because they attain freedom."1.

Richard Epstein, The Mother of Songs, states that "Premodern civilizations not only incorporated the animal kingdom into their spiritual practices, but worshipped them. The animal kingdoms represented the gods; when each species was the highest on the evolutionary ladder before the emergence of humankind. Even after highly evolved civilizations, i.e., Egypt, continued to venerate them in their animal forms. At least symbolized in Pharaoh Egypt in zoomorphic shapes. Writes Epstein, "The incarnation has the capacity of appearing before His/Her devotees in any shape or manner He or She chooses. Thus, in Paleolithic and Neolithic periods, the Divine Mother appeared before less tutored civilizations in misshapen physiques – half man, half animal, because that appearance was the most acceptable in accordance with their tribal understanding. The ancient Hindus could easily relate to elephant and monkey gods. Ganesha was a talking elephant long before Disney's Dumbo appeared on the scene. Likewise, in the scale of evolution, the avatars appeared to the highest form on earth whether in the body of a fish or any other being on the ascended scale of the evolutionary ladder in their respective forms. When John Blofeld [Bodhisattva of Compassion] asked a member of Ta Hai's (Chinese pundit) group about the fact that many Pure Land followers preferred Kuan Yin to Amitabha Buddha [multi-headed, multi-armed god] as their chosen idam (spiritual ideal), he was answered, 'Like you. They feel drawn to her. It is because of your nature. If you were a horse, you would be sure to invoke the Horse-Headed Hayagriva, who is also Kuan Yin. If a lobster, you would choose a lobster deity, just as Nagas invoke serpent divinities. Picturing compassion in the form of a lovely woman is a reasonable thing to do. Amitabha Buddha is compassion seen as a noble quality, shining and majestic. Kuan Yin is compassion seen as intimate and a counterpart of gentle pity. Not having many heads in the Indian manner, nor necessarily sharing Amitabha's vastness, she appeals to humanists like you and me and fits in well with our Chinese conception of divinity.'"2.

Standing Bear explains the Lakota's relationship to the animal kingdom. "Now the medicine-man derived his knowledge from the infinite source – Wakan-Tanka as manifested in the creatures and beings of nature. This association of knowledge with all the creatures of earth caused him to look to them for his knowledge, and assuming their spiritual fineness to be of the quality of his own, he sought with them a true rapport. If a man could prove to some bird or animal that he was a worthy friend, it would share with him precious secrets and there would be formal bonds of loyalty never to be broken; the man would protect the rights and life of the animal, and the animal would share with the man his power, skill and wisdom. In this manner was the great brotherhood of mutual helpfulness formed, adding to the reverence for life orders other than man...By acknowledging the virtues of other beings, the Lakota came to possess them for himself, and for his wonder and reverence, and for his unsurpassed humbleness and meekness Wakan Tanka revealed himself to the medicine man."3. "The white man laughs at the 'magic' of the Indian, that is because he does not understand the Indian's touch with nature."4.

Some of the Lakota dances were named and dedicated to certain animals, showing his love for and dependence upon the animal kingdom, such as the Fox, Horse, and Buffalo dances.

Vivekananda agrees, "We may worship anything by seeing God in it, if we can forget the idol and see God there. We must not project any image upon God. But we may fill any image with that Life which is God. Only forget the image, and you are right enough – for 'out of Him comes everything.' He is everything."5.

Ohiyesa informs us of the Sioux's attitude toward the universe in terms of his or her belief that "all living creatures in the universe are relatives." The animal kingdom and its association with the Indians was especially close. Ohiyesa explains, "Our first ancestor roamed happily among the animal people, who were in those days a powerful nation. He learned their ways and their language – for they had a common tongue in those days...notwithstanding that he was a good comrade and did them no harm."6.

Leonard Crow Dog expands, "We have been a relation-making tribe from the very beginning. All our ceremonies, a sweat or a vision quest, end the words 'Mitakuye Oyasin' 'all my relations' – and that means every living being on this earth down to the tiniest bug or flower. Everything that lives is related. The hunka lowanpi is part of this life philosophy."7. Lame Deer credits the Holy Woman for inspiring this attitude.

Vivekananda gives us a Vedic insight which correlates with the hunka Iowanpi. "All are our fellow passengers, our fellow travelers – all life, plants, animals; not only my brother man, but my brother brute, my brother plant; not only my brother the good, but my brother the evil, my brother the spiritual and my brother the wicked. They are all going to the same goal. All are in the same stream, each is hurrying towards that infinite freedom."8.

Ohiyesa continues the mythical allegory about the powwow between species. From his account, the harmonious relationship went south, when an anthropomorphic insect disrupted the normal course of things and joyfully sparked adversity between friends. "Only with the coming of Unk-to-mee, the Spider was the harmonious relationship ruptured." Possibly Ohiyesa is referring to Iktomi, the creature held in ambivalence among the Lakota whom we have seen before. Iktomi is known as the trickster.

The Spider turned the animal kingdom against humankind. Unk-to-mee once more sowed dissension among the animals, and messages went out into all quarters of the earth that all tribes might unite to declare war upon the solitary man destined to become their master.

A while later "First Born" of the Sioux created Little Boy Man from a splinter drawn from his great toe and made him his brother. The latter, not fully grown was a trusting and innocent child, discovered Unk-to-mee's plot. He returned to his abode in a downcast mood, due to his love for his friends, the animals. Thus, First Born, less sentimental than his younger brother, gave Little Boy Man the tools of combat: a bow and flint-headed arrows, a stone war-club and a spear. First Born, in addition created a wall of rock around the family tipi, and commanded his younger brother

to assert his supremacy and fight the animals that he blamed
for starting the war.

Little Boy Man obeyed and took refuge behind the wall,
"and at last he beheld the prairies, black with buffalo herds,
and the elk gathering upon the edges of the forest. Bears and
wolves were closing in from all directions, and now from the
sky the Thunder gave his fearful war-whoop, answered by
the wolf's long howl." For the first time on earth aggression
between the species resulted at the wall; Little Boy Man
was at his most skillful. He strung the bow and launched
hundreds of flint-headed arrows which found their mark in
the bodies of the animals. Each time the little warrior swung
his stone war-club, countless animals fell to the ground.

The dumb-founded animals sadly agreed to sue for peace.
The treaty rendered them as food for humans and the
additional humiliation of having to surrender their skins to
be made into clothing. But the treaty did not automatically
stipulate that the humans could overpower their prey
without some danger and a lot of effort. The insects stood
firm, bolting at the idea of complete capitulation. "Ever
since [they have been] tormentors of man; however the birds
of the air declared that they would punish them for their
obstinacy, and this they continue to do to this day."9.

The Powwow Among Relatives

In time the Sioux went beyond mere tolerance toward their
defeated subjects that had been exploited for the value they
served in maintaining the basic life-sustaining materials
of human existence. Tolerance changed into the kind of
acceptance Vivekananda spoke about. The animals were
not only embraced but were adopted as beloved relatives.
The buffalo and eagle held a special place in the pantheon.
The Indians respected all kinds of animals for the adept
wisdom they dispensed during vision quests and during

healing ceremonies, when the animals' secret knowledge proved indispensable to the outcome of saving lives. The practioners of medicine power did not hesitate to call for their assistance. Says Standing Bear, "There was a close brotherhood between the animal and the bird. So close did some of the Lakotas come to their feathered and furred friends that in true brotherhood they spoke a common tongue."10.

St. Pierre and Long Soldier declare that movements of animals like the buffalo were at times guided by proper communication between the Lakota and the spirits of the animals they depended upon for food. Special men and women, who had dreams of these animals became sacred interpreters and petitioners to these animal grandfather spirits and, thus, became shamans.

At the cave of Amarnath in the Himalayas, Vivekananda answers a disciple's statement about three or four white pigeons frequenting the cave, and the mere sight of these birds being indicative of being blessed with the vision of Shiva. The Swami answered, "I have heard the sight of the pigeons brings to fruition – whatever desires you may have."11.

The Eagle, at the pinnacle of the bird species, had all the attributes of humankind, and, according to Wallace Black Elk could unleash vengeance even from the spirit world. The Indians would not be surprised that even an eagle could redress the wrongdoing of a predator who had shot him to death for the hell of it. The bird's spirit visited Black Elk and informed him, "Now a wasichu [white man] put me on target for no reason at all. But I am a spirit. I'm sacred. In four days you shall see."

One day Black Elk found the wounded eagle lying on the road with a broken wing; he had been shot out of his perching place. Black Elk chewed a piece of sage and plugged the bird's wounds. According to Lame Deer, all sage is sacred to the Lakota. "It is our 'first aid' plant, and we use it in all our ceremonies. It represents the power of nature."

After applying the sage, Black Elk made a splint for his broken wing, picked him up and prayed to the west, but the eagle died anyway. Black Elk took the dead bird's claws and vowed to pierce himself with them during the Sun Dance. Afterward the gratified eagle reminded him that the spirit's vow would be fulfilled in four days. Four days later, Black Elk reported, "I was going along the same road where I had found that eagle. I saw a pickup along the road, and two elders were standing there. I stopped and got out. This man was laying there dead along side a rifle. Those old people saw this man stop his pickup. There was an eagle sitting there on this haystack, and he got out of the pickup to shoot that eagle. His rifle was lying on the front seat. He pulled back and forth on his rifle by the barrel, and it went off. It shot him through in the same place the eagle had been shot through. So I knew it was the same man. So four days later, I saw this, and it was sacred."12.

On the other hand, the animal can have the compassion of a bodhisattva. Leonard Crow Dog tells a story of the coyote's contribution as a reconnaissance scout on the battlefield. Leonard cites the coyote for having been instrumental in saving the life of Henry Crow Dog, his grandfather, during one of the wars with the Crow tribe. Henry was so grateful that he changed his name to Crow Coyote because, "The coyote was my grandfather's sacred animal. It has to do with wounds he received in a fight. Without the coyote he would have died, and it would all have ended right there."13.

Henry Crow Dog was struck with two enemy arrows in the midst of battle, one below the collarbone and one in his side.

As a large part of the pointed arrow remained in his body, he fell off his horse and believed death was staring him in the face. After crawling beneath some stinkwood bushes, he blacked out. "Then he heard the coyote whooping, Huuuuh, Crow Dog I'm coming human being, listen, I'm coming over.

"Pretty soon that coyote came and cuddled up to Crow Dog and warmed him. He whooped like one coyote speaking to another, 'Huuuuh, Crow Dog, I've come to doctor you. I brought you a special kind of sage. Pick it up. Doctor yourself with it.' Crow Dog had the wolf and coyote power. He could understand their language, understand it spiritually. Then a second coyote came and then a third, finally the fourth..." Other coyotes brought the wounded man Taopi Tawote, a healing substance. After the animal chewed the herb into mush, Crow Dog put it on the spot where the arrow had pierced him. The flesh was so soft he could pull out the arrow point. This was applied to his other wounds which healed rapidly. On the fourth day the coyotes convinced the wounded warrior that he could walk. "They talked among themselves and Crow Dog understood them. And they whooped, indicating that he should follow them. The coyotes scouted ahead for Crow Dog, warning him if enemies were close by. These coyotes were Wakan. A message from such a sacred coyote could reach New York faster than a telegram."14.

The Lakota powwowed with the animal kingdom because the animal was in tune with the gods, and for the Lakota and the Sioux they provided guidance and assistance in all matters, and endeavored to ensure affinity through offering fetishes and military dances. Even the communal dances of the Oglala involved love and appreciation for particular animals in the animal realm, which the Lakota depended upon: Lodges were built around the persona of certain animals like the Fox Lodge whose members expressed their appreciation for this little creature's nimbleness and the effects of his curing powers.

Stories and parables in the Upanishads bear a striking resemblance to the Lakota's Vedic relationship to the animal kingdom. Swami Vivekananda reveals an account of what Satyakama learned from the animal kingdom mentioned in the an allegory of the Chhandogya Upanishad: Satyakama went to a sage to learn the truth about the Vedas. The teacher gave Satyakama four hundred lean, weak cows to care for, and sent him to the forest. The sage told him to return when the herd would increase to a thousand. After a few years, one day Satyakama heard a big bull in the herd say to him, "We are a thousand now; take us back to your teacher. I will teach you a little of Brahman…The East is a part of the Lord, so is the West, so is the South, so is the North. The four cardinal points are the four parts of Brahman." Fire was a great symbol in those days, and every student had to procure fire and make offerings. So on the following day, Satyakama started for his guru's house, and when he had performed his oblation, and worshipped at the fire…he heard a voice come from the fire, "O Satyakama." "Speak, Lord," said Satyakama. "O Satyakama, I am come to teach you a little of Brahman. This earth is a portion of that Brahman. The sky and the heaven are portions of it. The ocean is a part of that Brahman." Then the fire said that a certain bird would teach him something. Satyakama continued his journey and on the next day when he had performed his evening sacrifice a swan came to him and said, "I will teach you something about Brahman. This fire which you worship, O Satyakama, is part of that Brahman. The sun is a part, the moon is a part, the lightning is a part of that Brahman. A bird called Madgu will tell you more about it." The next evening that bird came, and Satyakama heard a similar voice. "I will tell you something about Brahman. Breath is a part of Brahman, sight is a part, hearing is a part, and the mind is a part." Then the boy arrived at his teacher's place and presented himself before him with due reverence.

As soon as the guru encountered his disciple he remarked, "Satyakama, thy face shines like that of a knower of Brahman. Who then has taught thee?" "Beings other than men," replied Satyakama, "but I wish that you should teach me, sir. For I have heard from men like you that knowledge which is learnt from a guru alone leads to supreme good." Then the sage taught him the same knowledge which he had received from the gods. "And nothing was left out, yea, nothing was left out."15.

Swamiji points out that Satyakama's experiences with the animals or gods was coming from inside himself. "Now, apart from allegories of what the bull, the fire, and the birds taught, we see the tendency of the thought and the direction in which it was going in those days. The great idea of which we see the gem is that all these voices are inside ourselves. As we understand these truths better, we find that the voice is in our own heart, and the student understood that all the time he was hearing the truth; but his explanation was not correct. He was interpreting the voice as coming from the external world, while all the time, it was within him... and this is the practical side of Vedanta. It does not destroy the world, but explains it...it does not destroy the person, but explains him; it does not destroy the individuality but explains it by showing the real individuality. It does not show that this world is vain and does not exist, but it says, 'Understand what this world is, so that it may not hurt you.' The truth was shown through everything with which [Satyakama] was familiar...Everything became transformed and deified. Their real nature was known. The theme of the Vedanta is to see the Lord in everything, to see things in their real nature, not as they appear to be."16.

Modern demographers claim that every fifthteen years the world's population will increase by a billion human beings. Vivekananda states that the natural evolutionary process, whereby the animals' jiva transmigrates into higher and higher physical forms as it gathers expanded experiences and succeeds to higher manifestations of its real nature – God or the Atman – has been disrupted by humankind's incessant technology and its flagrant disregard for lower forms of life. "The animal is a state of sojourn for the Jiva evolving from lower forms. In course of time the animal becomes man. It is a significant fact that as the human population is increasing, the animal population is decreasing. The animal souls are all becoming men. So many species of animals have become men already. Where else have they gone?"17.

Wakan:
Deifying The Universe

Huaca in the Peruvian (Native American) canon implies a kind of pantheism. It is a name applied to anything of outstanding beauty, to objects ugly and monstrous, or those that inspire honor and alarm, anything out of the ordinary: a woman bearing twins for example, and the festive ceremony given to the bearer of twins to pay homage to her fecundity.

Most Native Americans strove to make religion the cornerstone of their lives. Observances of spiritual matters subtly penetrated every nuance of even the most mundane activity: the sowing and reaping of crops, the preparation of daily meals, all family events including birth, marriage, and death, barter and trade, the buffalo hunt, and the roles of both sexes were intertwined with the immanent presence and interposition of the deity.

The Huaca bears a likeness to the Wakan Tanka of the Sioux bands. Everything Wakan is sacred. The Dakota says that we do not see the real earth or rocks, only the Son-Wanpi of each. Writes Joseph Epes Brown, The Sacred Pipe, "It is notable that to the Plains Indian, the material form of the symbol is not conceived as representing a higher reality or substitute for another form, but is the actual reality in an image. The power or quality of being transferred directly to the person in contact with it, and there is no need, as with modern Western people for any mental or artificial reconstruction. It even goes so far as to enable the Indian to become one with its reflected power. Says [Nick] Black Elk, 'When we use water in the sweat lodge we should think of Wakan-Tanka who is always flowing, giving His power and life to everything; we should even be as water, which is lower than all things, yet stronger than rocks.'"1.

Ramakrishna notes that the, "Ever pure Brahman has been transformed into the Ganges to purify all beings. So the Ganges is truly Brahman in the form of water. The minds of all who live on the banks of the Ganges become divine, and the spiritual inclinations of these people manifest spontaneously. The air filled with the moisture of the Ganges purifies the land as far as it flows. The people who live in that area are endowed with good conduct, devotion to God, steadfastness, generosity, and austerity by the grace of the Ganges, the daughter of the great Himalayas."2.The Paramahamsa did not mean that all those inhabitants would be conferred with sainthood, but would have their spiritual practices enhanced in the same way that visiting sacred shrines benefits pilgrims and residents receive the grace of residing in holy places.

The Lakota says, "Mni (water) is essential and seen as

connecting all life. It is viewed as having sacred powers of healing. Water is used in conjunction with almost all ceremonies as the most precious and basic of gifts."3.

Wallace Black Elk describes how the Earth People, the Oglala, find joy and peace in a bubbling brook. "When this Earth Man goes to a bubbling brook he just sits there and drinks and admires. He listens to that wind whistling through the green and talks about the beautiful sounds made by the winged-people and all of life. That is the philosophy of the Earth people. But if a scientist goes to that same place, the first thing he will think of is how to make that 'damn' water work for him. He'll want to put a dam there and a high turbine generator. But the Earth Man will just sit there and listen to that bubbling brook and the wind. So that is our philosophy."4.

And Vivekananda, "A current rushing down of its own nature falls into a hollow and makes a whirlpool, and after running a little in that whirlpool, it emerges again in the form of the free current to go on unchecked. Each human life is like that current. It gets into the whirl, gets involved in this world of space, time, causation, whirls round a little crying out, 'My father, my brother, my name, my fame,' and so on, and at last emerges out of it and regains its original freedom. The whole universe is doing that. Whether we know it or not, whether we are conscious or unconscious of it, we are all working to get out of the dream world. Man's experience in the world is to enable him to get out of its whirlpool"5.

Swami quotes from the Upakosala Karmalayana scriptures, which explains that the elements of nature are one and the same as Brahman. " 'This earth, food, fire and sun; whom you worship, are forms of Brahman. The person that is seen in the sun; I am He. Who knows this and meditates on Him, all his sins vanish and he has long life and becomes happy.

He who lives in the cardinal points, the moon, the stars, and the water, I am He. He who lives in this life, the ether, the heavens and the lightening, I am He.'"6.

The Native American's devotion to the sun is rational when seen in the context of the Wakan concept. Evans-Wentz gives a plausible explanation for the Indians' continued reverence for this object. "The Indian no more worshiped the Sun than the Christian does the Cross. The Sun and the Earth, by an obvious parable, holding scarcely more poetic metaphor than of the scientific truth, were in his view the parents of all organic life. From the Sun, as the universal Father, proceeds the quickening principle of nature, and in the patient and fruitful womb of our Mother, the Earth, are hidden embryos of plants and men. Therefore our reverence and love for them was really an imaginative extension of our love for our immediate parents; and with this sentiment of filial piety was joined a willingness to appeal to them, as to a father, for such good gifts as we may desire. This is the material or physical prayer."7.

All metaphors aside, Standing Bear's point of view is more to the point. "The Lakota did not worship the sun, nor did they pray to it. They merely recognized the bearing it had upon all life, manifesting as it did the universal powers of the Great Mystery. So when the Lakota prayed or sang songs of praise, the sun carried them direct to Wakan-Tanka.

"Every day for the Lakota began with a salute to the sun, and as a bringer of light, it was recognized, whether its face was visible or whether it was hidden by a clouded sky. It was habit and custom to receive the sun by awaiting its coming. For a moment, silently and erect, the sun was faced. There was no kneeling, no words were spoken, and no hands were raised, but in every heart was just a thought of tribute."8.

Even the most inanimate objects are conscious, living

sparks of divinity, since everything is God in the mind of the Sioux. Holy Mother makes this clear: even a broomstick deserves respect. "One morning while the Holy Mother was rubbing her body with oil, someone was sweeping the courtyard. After the work was all done, that person threw the broomstick aside. At this the Mother said, 'What is this? You have thrown away the broomstick with such disrespect when the work is done. It takes only the same length of time to put it gently in a corner as it does to throw it aside. One should not trifle with a thing, though it may be very insignificant. If you respect a thing, the thing also respects you. Will you not again need that broomstick? Besides, it is also a part of this family. From that standpoint also, it deserves to be treated with respect. One should perform even an insignificant work with respect."9.

Wallace Black Elk tells a story of what happened to some ceremonial objects left at a sweat lodge after a vision quest. The objects in question were some venerated vestments torn to shreds by vandals, and the sacred tobacco ties were sliced to pieces lying on the floor. Black Elk says that after a person returns from a vision quest, it is customary to leave the robes at the site for four days. When Black Elk returned to the sweat lodge on the fourth day, he discovered lying dispersed on the ground the robes torn to pieces. Two robes were missing, the others mutilated. The lodge had been vandalized – all the legs of the altar broken, and the canvas covers ripped apart. The tobacco ties were sliced with a knife or razor blade.

The next year Wallace Black Elk and his party returned to the same spot for a vision quest. The religious paraphernalia – tobacco ties and robes had disappeared. "So we prayed," Black Elk said, "so I told them to go into that hole, into that arbor. Go in there and see. So they went inside. Those robes were all there hanging inside. Those tobacco ties were hanging in there also. Even those torn ones were in there that we had buried like the day we made them. So that was a mystery. So those robes and ties have a life. So there are a lot of things that we have to understand. You shouldn't worry, you should only trust the Great Spirit."10.

The Oglala even have respect for rocks and stones because they, too, are conscious and the Great Spirit is part of them.

In the Oglala view a medicine man could broach the line between animate and "inanimate." Therefore tribal belief held (and holds) that rocks are alive. In the sweat lodge they may be raised to consciousness, thus, the rocks could talk, and at times – as in the case of Ayers Rock in Australia, they may be understood as divine.

Hot stones reveal secrets beyond ordinary interaction of the senses. Says Standing Bear, "While taking the purification ceremony, the tunkes, or hot stones brought great inspiration to [Horn] Chips [a notable Lakota holy man], so when he went to the place of vigil they came to him in spirit and offered him service."11.

"Inyan – the rock – are holy," Lame Deer supports Standing Bear's statement. "Every man needs a stone to help him. There are two kinds of pebbles that make good medicine. One is white like ice. The other is like ordinary stone, but makes you pick it up and recognize it by its special shape. You ask stones for aid to find things which are lost or missing. Stones can give warnings of an enemy, of approaching misfortune. The winds are symbolized by a raven and a small black stone the size of an egg."12.

The Yuwipi ceremony is the power of the sacred rocks to heal a sick person. Lame Deer explains, "When a man skillful in the use of the sacred stones was called to attend a sick person he was expected to give a demonstration of his supernatural power. Many were invited to witness this exhibition, and it is said that harm would come to those who did not 'believe in the sacred stones.' The sick person filled a pipe, which he gave to the medicine man. After smoking it the man was tightly bound with thongs, even his fingers and toes being interlaced with sinews like those of which bowstrings are made, after which he was firmly tied in a hide. The tent was dark, and the medicine man sang songs addressed to the sacred stones; he sang also his own dream songs. Strange sounds were heard in the darkness, and objects were felt to be flying through the air. Voices of animals were speaking. One said, 'My grandchild, you are very sick, but I will cure you.' Frequently a buffalo came, and those who did not believe in the sacred stones were kicked by the buffalo or struck by a flying stone or bundle of clothing. At last the medicine man called, 'Hasten, make a light!' Dry grass, which was ready, was placed on the fire. In the light the man was seen wedged between the poles near the top of the tipi, with all the restraining cords cast from him."13.

Medicine stone, according to Lame Deer, consists of the work of the Great Spirit, its surface has no beginning and no end.

The Manu Samhita – an ancient Indian treatise on religious law and social obligation declares, "Consciousness exists even in insentient things like trees and stones, and they experience happiness and misery also." (Manu Samhita, 1:49)

After a vision of the Divine Mother, Ramakrishna said, "If this vision of mine is true, let this rock [which was in front of the nahabat] jump three times." The rock actually jumped.14.

And Vivekananda states, "When the heart has been opened,

it becomes fit to receive the teaching from the stones or the brooks, the stars, or the sun, or the moon, or from any thing which has its existence in our universe."15.

The Little Brother of the Four Winds: Prana

Many people confuse prana with breath, but according to Vedanta and Native America, Prana is not breath, but the power that moves the lungs. Prana is the vital force pervading the entire universe and allows innumerable objects physical motion. It is invisible but the force behind the winds, even a hurricane. Every human being and animal has a ration of this force within allowing it to live and move about; in humans even thought has Prana as its cause. Swami Vivekananda explains the force of prana in the universe. "[Out of this Prana, everything that we call energy and force is evolved]. It is the Prana that is manifesting as motion; it is the Prana that is manifesting as gravitation, as magnetism. It is Prana that is manifesting as the actions of the body, as the nerve currents, as thought force. From thought down to the lowest force, everything is but a manifestation of Prana."1.

In the Navajo version, Prana is a spiritual entity that gives life, thought, speech and movement to all living elements. The "Holy Wind" exists all around and within the individual. It enters and departs through the respiratory organs and surface of the body. It directs the movements of the body and leaves the body at death. The Vedic view is that at the moment of death it is wholly concentrated in the individual's mind, i.e., the subtle body which survives the death of the gross physical and moves through innumerable cycles of samsara: birth, death, rebirth.

The Lakota believe that Wakan Tanka breathed life into all objects, visible and invisible. In the Lakota language Prana is called Skan.

Anthropologist, William Powers, adopted in boyhood by a Lakota chief and spent 35 summers on the Pine Ridge reservation lends clarity to the subject, " Skan, an abbreviation of Takuskanskan 'something that moves', a term which approximates the notion of a creation life force that causes the wind to blow. This term is best understood as that aspect of Wakan-Tanka that is creative, original. Another term is yumini, the name designating the little brother of the Four Winds who never grows up and who is never assigned a direction. The little brother most frequently lives and travels with the South Wind who is kind to him. Yumini is an unusual form of attenuation; it is short for Wamniomini 'whirlwind', usually referring to the small dust devil that skips about the prairie."2.

The Dakota believe spiders, bisons, birds, flying insects and even cottonwood trees have a unifying relationship, for each one reveals a special tie to the wind or breath. The wind moves exerting power over natural forms but remains unseen; it is the Great Mystery in a metaphorical sense in that its invisible presence gives life and movement to all that is. The winds are anthromorphized and identified with the four directions.

Wallace Black Elk describes the Skan as the breath of spirit. "It remains here, because the wisdom [from Tunkashila] and knowledge [from Grandmother] were placed here. It doesn't go anywhere; it just stays right here.

"So the spirit that we are talking about, it is a great mystery. Like this air. It is here. You can see it moving the grass and leaves around. You can feel it, but you can't see it with your naked eyes. But it's here, and we are all breathing it, whether it's a black man or red man or yellow man or white man or winged, four-legged, creeping-crawler, mammal, or fish people. We are all breathing the same air. So that's just an example of how spirit goes back to spirit. This is the way it was told. So I pray this wind will blow away piece by piece those bad thoughts coming our way."3.

The Skan also enters the Lakota creation story of Iyan, the rock. "The energy given up by the rock, now hard and powerless, is Takuskan Skan, that which moves all things. This power was now diffused into the female earth, the male sky and the waters."4. Skan, who was the judge of all force and power, sat in judgment of all gods and spirits.

Crazy Horse, the great Oglala warrior, had a vision as told by Nick Black Elk. "Crazy Horse dreamed and went into the world where there is nothing but the spirits of all things. That is the real world that is behind this one, and everything we see here is something like a shadow from that world. He was on his horse in that world, and the horse and himself on it, and the trees and the grass and the stones and everything were made of spirit, and nothing was hard, and everything seemed to float. His horse was standing still there, and yet it danced around like a horse made only of shadow, and that is how he got his name, which does not mean that his horse was crazy or wild, but that in his vision it danced around in that queer way.

"It was this vision that gave him his great power, for when he went into a fight he had only to think of that world to be in it again, so that he could go through anything and not be hurt."5.

All Yuwipi spirits human and animal are in fact the spirits of those who once lived on earth. Hence, the Oglala feel a sense of continuity between the living and non-living, and enforces their belief that the spirit world is merely an extension of the earth world reinforced.

Vivekananda believes that seeing and communicating with departed souls is not the exclusive prerogative of spiritualists, who can communicate with them without departing this world, because a highly evolved soul, adept in yogic practice can duplicate the experiences of Crazy Horse and the Cowanpi priestess by ratcheting up his or her Prana or the vital life force pervading the entire universe. Says the Swami, "If it be true that the departed spirits exist, only we cannot see them, it is quite probable that there may be hundreds and millions of them about us we can neither see, feel, nor touch. We may be continually passing and repassing through their bodies, and they do not see or feel us. It is a circle within a circle, universe within universe. We have five senses, and we represent Prana in a certain state of vibration. All beings in the same state of vibration will see one another, but if there are beings who represent Prana in a higher state of vibration, they will not be seen. We may increase the intensity of a light until we cannot see it at all, but there may be beings with eyes so powerful that they can see such light. Again, if its vibrations are very low, we do not see a light, but there are animals that may see it, as cats and owls. Our range of vision is only one plane of the vibrations of this Prana.

"Think of the universe as an ocean of ether, consisting of layer after layer of varying degrees of vibration under the action of Prana; away from the centre the vibrations are less, nearer to it they become quicker and quicker; one order of vibrations makes one plane. Then suppose these ranges of vibration are cut into planes, so many millions of miles one set of vibrations, and then so many millions of miles another still higher set of vibrations and so on. It is, therefore, probable that those who live on the plane of a certain state of vibration will have the power of recognizing one another, but will not recognize those above them. Yet just as by the telescope and the microscope we can increase the scope of our vision, similarly we can by Yoga bring ourselves to the state of vibration of another plane, and thus, enable ourselves to see what is going on there. Suppose this room is full of beings whom we do not see. They represent Prana in a certain state of vibration while we represent another. Suppose they represent a quick one, and we the opposite. Prana is the material of which they are composed, as well as we. All are parts of the same ocean of Prana, they differ only in their rate of vibration. If I can bring myself to the quick vibration this plane will immediately change for me: I shall not see you anymore; you vanish and they appear. All this bringing of the mind into a higher state of vibration is included in one word in Yoga – Samadhi. All these states of higher vibration, super consciousness vibration of the mind, are grouped in that one word, Samadhi, and the lower states of Samadhi give us vision of these beings. The highest grade of Samadhi is when we see the real thing, when we see the material out of which the whole of these grades of beings are composed, and that one lump of clay being known, we know all the clay in the universe."6.

Medicine Power

Nick Black Elk explains that the ceremonial (sweat) lodge has a lesson to teach humankind in the realization of the inner-self. "For in the fall [the trees] leaves die and return to the earth, but in the spring they come to life again. So, too, men die but live again in the real world of Wakan-Tanka, where there is nothing but the spirit of all things; and this true life we may know here on earth, if we purify our bodies and minds, thus coming closer to Wakan-Tanka who is all purity."1.

The ceremony itself is a method of purifying the mind and body of the participants. Again Black Elk, "During the four periods of Sweating within the lodge, prayers are recited, sacred songs are sung, and a pipe is ceremonially smoked four times by the circle of people. At the conclusion of the fourth and last period, the door is opened so that the 'light enters into darkness, that we may see not only with our two eyes, but with the one eye which is of the heart, and with which we see and know all that is true and good.' Going forth into the light from the house of darkness in which all impurities have been left behind, represents human liberation from ignorance, from the ego, and from the Cosmos. The person is now a renewed being, entering symbolically into the world of light and wisdom."2. Chapter 20 covers this subject more thoroughly.

According to Patanjali (Yoga Sutras 111,41) by controlling the force, i.e., sexual energy, which governs the Prana (vital force behind everything in the universe), the disciple acquires the power to surround the body with a blaze of light. This bares a likeness to the Orenda (Iroquois), Wakan (Sioux) and Manitou experienced by certain medicine men or shamans and other yogic practitioners within the Native American fold.

In the Sioux experience the Wakan is impersonal force, or magic power, "assumed to be inherent in everybody or being in nature. It is a dynamic energy associated with all natural phenomena affecting mankind's welfare, although limited in its function and efficacy, local rather than omnipresent, and objectively embodied. Its possession is a distinctive characteristic of all deities."3.

The power of the shaman, according to Vivekananda, comes from tapas. "Tapas means literally 'to burn.' It is a kind of penance to 'heat' the higher nature. It is sometimes in the form of a sunrise to sunset vow, such as repeating Om all day incessantly. These actions will produce a certain power that you can convert into any form you wish, spiritual or material."4.

The Wakan conceived by the Sioux is the term medicine

power known to other native peoples. Medicine power is related to personal prowess, "which in the (individual's understanding) is not dissociated from power of thought and order of knowledge; physical and mental are, as it were, one breath of being, magical in its action, so that at the core of every potency, whether of muscular skill or sagacious conduct, there is a single essential force. This is what is termed 'medicine' power in relation to Indian usage, and it is the quest of such medicine that a great portion of the life-career of the Indian was devoted."5. Leonard Crow Dog affirms, "A medicine man lives among his people. He has to experience life, all of it. He must be higher than an eagle and, sometimes, lower than a worm. He exists for the people and he has to fight for them if necessary. He must even turn himself into a politician if a politician is what his people need."6.

The medicine man, therefore, was and is a man of great attainment. He/she was (and is) the healer of the sick, and he administers the arts of divination. The "medicine societies" are a class within a class, highly respected with a special function in the tribal economy: surgeons, rain priests, guardians of seed corn and sacred objects.

The medicine power for many Indians is the essence of dealing with the ordeal of life through reliance upon individual visions as the fundamental guiding force. Tribal rituals are secondary to personal visions. The emphasis is on the personal rather than the communal. Tribal rituals often relied on the vision of an individual who gingerly transmitted his knowledge to carefully selected individuals. Writes Hartley Burr Alexander, The World's Rim, "Even in the great food-winning ceremonies such as the game and war dances, while these are cosmically timed and set by nature, nevertheless in their mythic backgrounds is invariably recognized some personal adventure or sacrifice: some seer adventuring the wilderness that he may bring thence the secret teaching of the gods that will lure forth the food-animals…the ritual is only the outer and incidental setting for the man's self-proof and inward vision. Throughout the central conception is dualistic and dramatic; the natural world and the social provide the scene and the spectacle, but in the man's soul is the action."7.

Besides the healing capacities, certain medicine men could prophesize future events, lost or hidden articles; hunters were assisted when the buffalo was compelled to go off course and to follow a tract in easy reach of a hunting party.

Discovering the future – allowing religious practitioners to predict the future in part or whole, to give advise on courses of action, and to give general advise and warnings on a variety of subjects – was, as Standing Bear said, once a major part of Lakota spirituality. "In the last two decades, said Deloria, " traditional healers have significantly increased the scope and depth of their ability to foretell the future. The impending earth catastrophes are appearing more and more in these rituals and this prospect had meant a great increase in the number of Indians returning to traditional ways. Unlike some Western efforts to predict specific personal fortunes, the information received by Indian religious leaders generally describes situations and conditions that are likely to come to pass, given existing circumstances. There is a sophisticated principle of probability here reminiscent of modern explanations of modern physics."8. Some shamans can localize and transfer medicine power. Like a simile of magnetizing iron, medicine power, either spontaneously or through magnetic and psychic radiations from human and non-human beings, makes a particular site magnetically and psychically effective for all animate entities that come within the parameters of its influence. "Every animate thing coming into birth adds its own Orenda to the collective total of the earth's Orenda."9.according to Evans Wentz.

While Swami Vivekananda cautions against the aspirants delving into the occult as heap bad medicine, he does, however, mark the validity of such experiences insofar as they are acquired through Raja Yoga (psychic control), a branch of yoga science respected in India and recently has swept the West off its feet. In the course of his travels throughout India, Vivekananda encountered instances just as esoteric and arcane attributed to mental telepathy. The way such occult events work, Swamiji explains, are through thought transference. One man's thought is manifested to someone else in a distant place. "With preparations – not by chance – a man wants to send a thought to another mind at a distance, and this other mind knows that a thought is coming, and he receives it exactly as it is sent out.

"In ordinary cases the thought is dissolved into ethereal vibrations. Firstly the vibrations go into the receiver mind's brain and become resolved into his own thoughts…Here is a dissolution of thought and there is a resolution of thought. It is a roundabout process. But in telepathy there is no such thing, it is direct."10.

Behind Raja Yoga is the concept that the mind of humankind contains extraordinary powers. There is a universal mind to which each individual's mind is a part. One mind is connected to all the others, and each mind wherever it is located is in communication with the whole world.

Among the Sioux and within other American Indian nations, the medicine man sings holy songs to achieve intimation that he will find holiness. The songs heighten the "dream-seeker's" awareness, thoroughly pure in body with a strengthened mind and spirit. The possessor of medicine power is endowed with the power to not only confront the spirit world consciously, but to pierce the sensory world of illusion or maya which veils the Great Mystery. And as the Eastern holy man intones his mantra and sings holy syllables to be in synch with the eternal sound of Om – the word that manifests God – the natural symbol, the matrix of all various sounds – the traditional Native American believes his magical songs will augment the power of his medicine. His music is his chief means of impressing his sense of need upon the powers and bringing them into communication with himself.

The Medicine Persons

Shamanism: sometimes referred to as "the world's first religion. All remaining forms of shamans believe that through drugs, specialized ritual, self denial, or a combination of these, a sacred altar can be created, a mysterious place and time in which direct communication with the spirit realm can be accomplished."1.

Shamanism: belief in an ordered spirit world, the Advaita conjunction with Vedanta that Everything is God, a soul that survives after death, and that communication with these spirits: plants, animal, and human – provides important information to the living. Medicine persons address all supernatural beings as "Grandfather."

With the assistance of music and dancing, the shaman would work himself into a state of ecstasy or enrapture. The

Lakota medicine man assumes the divine possesses him only because his experience is always accompanied with euphoric power. He has a sense of being alive and in motion; his prophecy is equated with the launching of rockets from the hands of the unseen being. Ecstasy proves a large part of his experience and power, for being in the hands of the spirit world, these men temporarily out run their human, physical limitations, and being in the hands of the Great Spirit, they can outrun the fastest ponies, and are caught up in the plains and cast on mountain tops. Through these prophets had/have a base among their own band and can receive the divine visitation while in solitude, in the same instance, it is claimed that the divine speak through them more clearly. No longer does the medicine man's experience manifest itself as an overpowering emotion only, but the emotion backs up the message delivered by the Great Spirit.

Sitting Bull of the Hunkpapa band, was said to be a holy man by many people; he had a vision during the Sun Dance. Writes Stanley Vestal, an Oglala scholar, "Black Moon walked out into the middle of the Sun Dance enclosure and called out in a loud voice: 'Sitting Bull wishes to announce that he heard a voice from above saying, 'I gave you these because they have no ears.' Actually he looked up and saw soldiers and some Indians on horseback coming down like grasshoppers with their heads down and their hats falling off. They were falling right into our camp."2. This was a vision which foretold the biggest victory of the Sioux and Cheyenne nations over the Seventh cavalry and the demise of General George Custer at the Little Big Horn river on June 25, 1876.

Sitting Bull warned his people, "These dead soldiers who are coming are the gifts of God. Kill them, but do not touch the spoils. If you set your hearts upon the goods of the white man, it will prove a curse to this nation."3

After the battle of the Little Big Horn, the victorious warriors stripped the dead, taking their weapons and ammunition, horses and clothing. Nick Black Elk relates a humorous incident regarding the theft of the enemies' clothes. "That evening everybody got excited and began shouting: 'The soldiers are coming!' I looked, and there they were riding abreast right toward us. But it was some of our own men dressed in the soldiers' clothes. They were doing this for fun."4. But the victory over Custer was short-lived. A year later Crazy Horse was assassinated at Fort Robinson where he was tricked into surrendering, and Sitting Bull fled into Canada with some of his band.

Sitting Bull heaved a sigh when he saw the fun makers. "Because you have taken the spoils, henceforth you will covet the white Man's goods, you will be at his mercy, you will starve at his hands." And he added, "The soldiers will crush you."5. Altogether the Indians had taken carbines and pistols of more than two hundred dead soldiers, and perhaps fifty rounds for each gun from the saddlebags and cartridge belts.

Clearing away the Hollywood stereotypes about the B movies medicine man, Standing Bear disclosed that the traditional, mainstream practitioner was simply a healer – curing, or attempting to cure the ailments endured by members of his people and had nothing to do with spiritual suffering. "A medicine man was no holier than other men, no more honored than a brave or a scout."6.

Other accounts, viz, Lame Deer, St. Pierre and Tilde Long Soldier, and most of our other narrators, believe that medicine power is derived from Wakan-Tanka, the infinite source; through rigorous sadhana, as we have seen, many shamans acquired the unique power they possessed. The traditional medicine man, Standing Bear concedes acquired the wisdom of the animal kingdom, and his rapport with a bird or another species of the animal world formed a bond never ruptured: the man would shield the rights and life of a particular animal and was reciprocated with the animal's skill, power, and wisdom. The animal is endowed with protean powers to change into other animals and even human beings. In his lamenting vision, Nick Black Elk saw a cloud of beautiful butterflies of every color and description. They swarmed around him in thick clusters; he was blinded and could see nothing else. "Then suddenly the butterflies changed and were storm driven swallows, swooping and whirling in a great cloud behind the charging riders."7.

Standing Bear admits that the spiritually gifted shaman was a cut above the mainstream. By accepting the virtue of the animal kingdom, he declares, the Lakota found it possible to possess these sources for himself. For the Lakota's humility, Wakan Tanka revealed him to the medicine man.

Visions came in dreams after the purification rites, the fast and vigil in solitude. The dumb creatures were enabled to converse with the medicine man. Many songs were dreamer songs obtained while in communion with the spirits of beings personified as humans. Dreamers who provided songs to the adepts were representative of the animal kingdom whose wisdom was imparted through song, which the medicine man disseminated to his people. The dreamer-animal relationship was a reciprocal street: the animal spirits learned from the human dreamer. For instance, the Bear Dreamer was told to use a bear claw as a healing aid and the recovery of the patient would be of short duration.

"Any dream that lingers upon waking is worth considering, pondering over, because to the Indian people, that dream is a means of the most essential communication with the spirit world."8. Many hopeful disciples of Ramakrishna had received their mantras in a dream.

For some diseases a fox would be the central player because of its knowledge of objects invisible to human eyes; the dreamer was advised to seek certain roots and herbs for the efficacy of treatment.

The Elk dreamer was popular with Lakota men seeking spouses. The Elk dreamer was relied on to protect the prospective husband and other men from the wiles of women seeking snares for unsuspecting members of the opposite sex. The Elk Dreamers were represented in ceremonies wearing deer masks and their bodies painted yellow. Warriors who went into battle, having sung the Brave song, met death fearlessly.

Mark St. Pierre and Tilda Long Soldier disclose that tribal women are called on to perform these sacred services to alleviate human suffering. "Beyond the childbearing years – beyond menopause – is when many opportunities open up for Lakota women, including the central one here, the calling to help those who are suffering. Whatever the woman's calling – to doctor through the spirit or with herbs, or to prophesy – this is when her powers become manifest, mature. It is the point in life into which all the women healers in this book, living and dead, passed before they became holy women. The dreams may have begun earlier, as might apprenticeship in ritual ways, but fulfillment was virtually always postponed until the woman was beyond childbearing and her awesome female powers had mellowed.

"Like men, Plains Indian women may be called to a number of distinct if occasionally overlapping roles in the spiritual service of their people. The term holy woman is as vague as the term healer. Native terms are much more complex and numerous than clichés like 'medicine man.' Understanding these names in the context of Indian people and the language they come from is critical to an accurate understanding of the approach and the role of the holy woman in her contact with the realm of the spirits."9.

THE WEAK SHALL WALK: SPIRITUAL HEALING

Nick Black Elk conducted his first healing in the summer of 1882. In response to a friend's entreaty for assistance in the healing of his ailing child, Black Elk undertook his first cure.

Cuts-to-Pieces, the child's father retrieved a pipe with an eagle feather on it. When he arrived with the pipe, Black Elk told him to take it around to the left of him, to leave it and pass out to the right of him. With the assistance of One Side, another friend, Black Elk carried the pipe to the tipi with the child inside. Joining him at the tipi were Black Elk's parents, and Standing Bear already there.

With the pipe offering to the six Grandfathers of Black Elk's childhood vision, the ritual began, and the medicine man and the close circle of bystanders, smoked the traditional red bark inside the bowl. Black Elk then made a rumbling sound like thunder on a drum that he brought with him and explained, "When the power of the west comes to the two-legged [humans], it comes with rumbling, and when it has passed everything lifts up its head and is glad and there is greenness…also the voice of the drum is an offering to the Spirit of the world. Its sound arouses the mind and makes men feel the mystery and power of things."10.

Black Elk proceeded to take his party to the northeast side of the tipi where the child lay, and they completed a circle from left to right. This, too, has a spiritual significance. The south is the source of life, and it is the provenance of the flowering stick; also the individual passes his life from there to the setting sun of his life. The individual must pass through the colder north (the direction of the white hairs) and if he survives, he passes through the east – the source of light and understanding. "Then does he not return to where he began, to his second childhood, there to give back his life to all life, and his flesh to the earth whence it came."

The sick child appeared to be merely skin and bones. At the sick bay, Black Elk had possession of the pipe, the drum, and a four-rayed herb: white, blue and yellow called the "Flower of Understanding", which he retrieved at Grass Creek beforehand. In addition to the pipe and drum – to complete the healing paraphernalia, Black Elk was given a wooden cup, filled with water, and an eagle- bone whistle – the spotted eagle which appeared in his childhood vision, which we shall take up in another chapter. Black Elk gave the whistle to One Side with instructions how to use it; the pipe was given to the daughter of Cuts-to-Pieces with instructions, "As I had seen the virgin of the east holding it in my great vision."

The following procedure was an appeal to the Spirit of the World – a cry of "Hey-a-a-hey", accompanied by a low thunder on the drum four times. "While I was doing this," said Black Elk, "I could feel the power coming through me from my feet up, and I knew that I could help the sick little boy."

Black Elk continued his drum beat and prayed to the Great Spirit, "My Grandfather, Great Spirit, you are the only one and to no other can any one send voices. You have made everything, and you have made it good and beautiful. The four quarters and the two roads crossing each other, you have made. Also you have set a power where the sun goes down. The two-leggeds on earth are in despair. For them, my Grandfather, I send a voice to you. You have said this to me: The Weak Shall Walk..."11.

As he continued his prayer to the Great Spirit, Black Elk explained the significance of the implements brought to the healing ritual: the four-rayed herb through its power will give the infirm the power to walk upright. The cup of water will allow the dying to live.

There is no dogma in Lakota tradition which makes orthodoxy of the implements brought by the medicine person to a healing ceremony. Blue Earring Woman of the Minnecojou used birds to "doctor" patients. Each bird would sing its song as it had in life. The equipment some practitioners use is chosen according to his or her dream. The most typical items appear to be: the pipe, a rawhide rattle, an eagle-bone whistle, a drum of various sizes, and a fan comprised of eagle feathers.

As Black Elk continued his prayer, he stated that a virgin will appear walking on the good Red Road; she will offer the pipe as she walks, and hers also is the power of the flowering tree. "From where the Giant lives (the north), you have given me a sacred, cleansing wind, and where this wind passes the weak shall have strength. You have said this to me. To you and to all your powers and to Mother Earth I send a voice for help."12.

Black Elk, untutored at his early age in the shaman arts – he was 19 – prayed to the west, and then walked to the north, to the east, and to the south, stopping at the good Red Road, the source of life. As Black Elk chanted his song in a "Sacred Manner", he felt a sudden surge of new energy throughout his body, "Something that made me want to cry for all unhappy things, and there were tears on my face."

As the ritual continues, there are more pipe oblations directed to the four quadrants. Black Elk recounts the culmination of the ceremony, which might be construed as the Lakota version of more conventional healing faiths, (Native American). "Next I took the cup of water, drank a little of it, and went around to where the sick little boy was. Standing before him, I stamped the earth four times. Then, putting my mouth to the pit of his stomach, I drew through him the cleaning wind of the north. I next chewed some of the herb and put it in the water, afterward blowing some of it on the boy and to the four quarters. The cup with the rest of the water I gave to the virgin [apparently the girl, who was part of Black Elk's prayer, had appeared in flesh and blood form] who gave it to the sick little boy to drink. Then I told the virgin to help the boy stand up and walk around the circle with him, beginning at the south, the source of life. He was very poor and weak, but with the virgin's help he did this."13. The boy recovered in four days, and according to Black Elk lived passed manhood. Black Elk said his healing power began after he performed the Heyoka (clown) ceremony.

Unlike many healers of other religious persuasions, Black Elk took no credit for himself; instead he was an intermediary (a channel) through which the power of the outer world, "and the visions and ceremonies had only made me like a hole through which the power could come to the two-leggeds. If I thought that I was doing it myself, the hole would close up and no power could come through. Then everything I could do would be foolish."14.

Vivekananda refers to the methods of healing utilized by the traditional practitioners, such as the medicine persons of Native America, as the manipulation of the Prana form of the practice of Pranayama: "Consciously or unconsciously health can be transmitted. A very strong man, living with a weak man, will make him feel a little stronger; whether he knows it or not. When consciously done this action becomes quicker and better. Next come those causes in which a person, though he may not be very healthy himself, yet can bring health to another. The first man, in such a case, has a little more control over his Prana, and for the time being can rouse his Prana to a certain state of vibration and transmit it to another person. It is the Prana that really does the curing. The faith-healer cures…because he brings the strength of his mind to bear upon the patient and rouses through faith, his dormant Prana."15.

One of the most astonishing examples of Native American healing is the power of Iktomi to heal patients especially with nervous disorders. We have encountered this little fellow in the Lakota allegory of maya where the spider trickster falls victim to his own snares. Many impartial readers may consider Wallace Black Elk's case study just more of his "hogie-pogie", but he is not shinning-on his non-Indian collaborators when he states, "The spider, we call him Iktomi; he walks, he rolls, he flies, and he sings a song. So we have medicine songs for that spider."16.

Black Elk renders an account of a paralyzed five-year-old child, cured by Iktomi's medicine in an up-to-date community hospital with state-of-the-art equipment, and doctors and nurses clothed in white. Black Elk, in curing the child, invoked Iktomi, the spider spirit. Iktomi diagnosed the illness: malfunction of the two nerves that branch out of the neck and interact with the brain, a knot was tied around one of the nerves; at the throat another knot was tied. The muscle in the throat, which contracts when a person swallows or uses his vocal cords, was also tied with a knot, hindering the contractions or release; the knots affected the power of the whole system. Medical science had no cure or instrument sophisticated enough to spot the web.

Conducting a healing ceremony right at the hospital ward,

the Indians sang the Iktomi calling song and the red spider, leader of all spiders, assisted the cure. Black Elk describes the proficiency of Iktomi. "So that red spider understood what I said. Then we sang a song. So he goes over to that little boy, and he untangles that web around his throat. He knows how because that's his web. So he could climb it. He knows about that because that is a part of him. That's part of his ingenuity.

"Then he came back and said, 'I took that web off. So that boy is going to educate his muscles now, and he is going to make sounds. So you are going to hear his voice now for the first time.'"17.

The Lakota party thanked Iktomi with the pipe song: "Oh, Tunkashila. The tobacco ties and robes we give you these. So touch them or take them."18. The spider accepted the offerings and departed. The upshot was the boy was cured – he ate and screamed like a normal five year-old, and the amazed doctor was unable to make out his reports, fearing a skeptical scientific world. "So he just wrote it down like it happened." A matter-of-fact Black Elk concludes, "Then the spider took off, then the boy was making sounds, then they fed him, and he ate and ate, then he was walking around, doing somersaults and all this."19.

St. Pierre and Long Soldier agree, "Spiders are common and powerful allies for spiritual doctoring."20.

The paradox between Inktomi (sic), the trickster and Iktomi, the healer is explained by William Powers. "Since Inktomi does take on so many different kinds of characteristics and personalities, one wonders why he should be called Inktomi and not by a name more befitting his reckless and immoral sojourns. The answer lies in the fact that the Lakota regard the spider as the wisest of all creatures, and part of this reasoning is based on observation of real spider behavior.

"According to Lakota medicine men...the spider is the most knowledgeable creature because he is the most ubiquitous, he lives and travels everywhere...spiders walk on the ground and walk underground. They can fly, and they can swim. They can be found anywhere, even in the most remote places, and there is nowhere a person can go without being seen or heard by spiders.

"Because of their ability to traverse the four important planes of Lakota cosmology – the sky and the clouds, the earth and beneath the earth – they are particularly knowledgeable about sacred things."21.

Even as far back as the 1930s, scientific-minded non-Indians in public health and elsewhere were beginning to recognize the efficacy of traditional tribal medical practices. Standing Bear gives his version of this open-mindedness. "Today healing remains one of the major strengths of tribal religions. Christian missionaries are unable to perform comparable healing ceremonies, and a great many still regard Indian healers as fakers and charlatans. This particular field is thus open for Indian religious figures who have received particular healing powers, and traditional healing ceremonies are being recognized by the Public Health Service as competent complementary healing practices. Some special grants have been given to train more healers and shamans, and to have them work closely with doctors trained in internal medicine."22.

HGMUGA: SORCERY

In Vedanta philosophy good and evil are relative terms intertwined, because within maya you cannot have one without the other. Swami Vivekananda leaves no room for doubt. "Objective society will always be a mixture of good and evil – objective life will always be followed by its shadow, death; and the longer the life, the longer will also be the shadow. It is only when the sun is on our head that there is no shadow. When God and good and everything else is in us, there is no evil. In objective life, however, every bullet has its billet – evil goes with every good as its shadow. Every improvement is coupled with an equal degradation. The reason being that good and evil are not two things but one, the difference being only in manifestation – one of degree, not kind."23.

Generally most Native Americans view disease in terms of spiritual causes relating to a person's failure to observe restrictions that govern correct behavior. Spirit possession or witchcraft; transgression of ceremonial rites and sorcery are also sources of illness and pathologies.

The Lakota believe that the medicine man's helpers are powerful yet neutral. Evil, as in Vedanta is a relative matter. Hgmuga is a Lakota word for witchcraft. A spirit helper assists the hgmuga, to cast a spell against an individual. As in Vedanta, the Lakota believe in karma – what goes around comes around – so the majority of practitioners give the hgmuga a wide berth.

The hgmuga ceremony, with prayers directed at doing harm to an enemy may boomerang against the family of the person unleashing those powers. If the curse is against a medicine man, the danger includes pollution, physical weakness and death.

The Lakota have their own version of Mother Kali; she is called Anukite' or Double-Face Woman. Her origin is linked to the Lakota creation legend. Simply she takes pleasure in punishing and taunting men. According to St. Pierre and Long Soldier, "She is still very dangerous to men and can influence women to be promiscuous as well as artistic."

White-tailed deer are believed to have a unique relationship to courting men; the deer are said to be manifestations of Anukite' influence.

Lucy Swan, a Lakota medicine woman explains this phenomenon. "We believe that certain women can appear to men as deer. Sometimes this can be dangerous. If a man is out hunting alone and sees a doe, he shouldn't follow her. They can be tricky. She might be a spirit deer and try to fool him. She will smell very attractive and might even appear to him as a beautiful young woman. She may make him follow her by using her deer perfume.

"He will follow her a long way, and when they stop to lie down together, she will turn back into a deer and run off. This will make him confused, crazy, and he could wander until he freezes or starves to death."24.

Another name used for her is Anung Ite. According to Lakota legend, Ite was possessed with beauty and charm. Absorbed in her beauty, Ite neglected her sons, the four winds. Sun was infatuated with Ite. Forgetting his wife, Hanwi, he invited Anukite' to sit beside him during the feast of the gods. Ite, who dared to preempt the place of a goddess, came before Shan who passed judgment on her. Shan passed a severe sentence on the beautiful Ite. In condemnation of her vanity and ambition, of her negligence of maternal and connubial duties, she would give premature birth to her next son, who would live with their father, Tate, and he would be ostracized by his childhood peers. In addition, Anukite' would be recycled back to earth and live as a solitary recluse. A crueler twist comes with this allegory of the Double-face Woman: a freakish appearance was her punishment: half her face incredibly beautiful, the other half, incredibly ugly; hence, everyone would be terrified by the sight of her. Yet she was not all evil. Anukite' made the first quilted robe, and she continues to influence Lakota female artisans.

Lucy Swan sums it up, "Double Woman Dreamers are considered bad, loose, or immoral, always chasing someone else's husband, and others are principally good, whereas a few have both aspects to their nature. 'If you dream of twins or are born a twin, you will be a good quill worker. Anukite' has this power to influence artists...a little girl born with two swirls on her head will be a good artist.'"25.

The Wicahmunga are contributors of misfortune. They explain calamities: accidents, murder, and sudden death of children. The medicine person predicts that certain unfavorable incidents are caused by evildoers, but can be mitigated through proper prayers and ceremonies.

Holy Mother explains that a sadhu or Vedanta sayassin (a monk or nun who has taken his or her final vows of monasticism) has the power of doing injury when spited by a householder. "A sadhu; you don't know that one word or thought of his may injure a householder. Whenever you see a sadhu, you should not show him disrespect by retorts or slighting remarks."26.

Nothing rings more true than Ramakrishna's experience with the water and his elder brother's curse. Holy Mother in one of her conversations noted, "Karma alone is responsible for our misery and happiness. Even the Master [Ramakrishna] had to suffer from the effects of karma. Once his elder brother was drinking water while delirious. The Master snatched the glass out of his hand after he had drunk just a little. The brother became angry and said, 'You have stopped me from drinking water. You will also suffer likewise. You will also feel such pain in your throat.' The Master said, 'Brother, I did not mean to injure you. You are ill. Water will harm you. That is why I have taken the glass away. Why have you then cursed me in this manner?' 'I do not know, brother.

These words have come from my mouth. They cannot but bear fruit.' At the time of his illness, the Master told me, 'I have this ulcer in my throat because of that curse.' I said to him in reply, 'How can man possibly live if such a thing as this can happen to you?' The Master remarked, 'My brother was a righteous man. His words must come true. Can the words of anyone and everyone be thus fulfilled?' The result of karma is inevitable. But by repeating the name of God you can lessen its intensity. If you were destined to have a wound as wide as a ploughshare, you will get a pinprick at least. The effect of karma can be counteracted to a great extent by japa and austerities."27.

But Ramakrishna's fatal disease – throat cancer – was not the result of an impetuous curse – and there were others -, but from taking upon himself the karma of others. Girish Gosh, a brash bohemian connected to the theatrical world, and all associated with it, was allowed wide leeway among Ramakrishna's inner circle because of his unshakable faith and devotion to his guru, Ramakrishna. Nevertheless, the Holy Mother told one disciple, "The Master used to say, 'I have all these physical ailments, because I have taken upon myself the sins of Girish [Gosh].'"28.

The mark of a spiteful sadhu surely finds its mark, but the vindication of the Chanunpa (sacred pipe) is heap bad medicine even for the offense of a bad thought. Wallace Black Elk warns that the Chanunpa is sensitive to a person's vibrations, especially bad thoughts, which can result in negative consequences for the thinker. "A lot of Christian people try to interpret God. They say God is love or love is God, like that. People don't really understand. That Chanunpa can destroy with that bad thought or bad word in there [the sacred lodge]. That is why I said that the spirit told me if a bad thought or bad word ever comes to you, to let it go in your ear and out the other ear, but never out of your mouth, it is going to hurt somebody, and then that hurt will come back to you twice. If you connect yourself to quick thought, that will take you someplace you'll never find your way back from. This was told many generations ago. So it was handed down. So when you have that Chanunpa, you have to be humble and sincere. You ask for health and help. Those are the key words that the Chanunpa carries."29. It is only when the bowl and stem of the pipe are joined that the pipe is powerful, even dangerous. When thus joined it is equated with a loaded gun and must be handled with acute respect for its potential.

Theft of the Pipe Bundle or anything associated with the Chanunpa would be summarily fatal for the offenders. A story told on the Cheyenne River Reservation took place in 1898, and would tend to substantiate Wallace Black Elk. "There were some five policemen [Lakota] involved in the theft of the Pipe Bundle, under the direction of the Indian agent couchman. Elk Head, ninth keeper of the Sacred Pipe Bundle, had possession. White Bull was a policeman at this time and was admired by the elders for his bravery and his fairmindedness. When the agent took the Pipe Bundle, a delegation of the Elk Head family went to see [Joseph] White Bull (nephew of Sitting Bull). He said he would go to see the agent and ask him to return the Bundle to the Indians.

"The agent agreed to do so, since his curiosity had been satisfied as to the contents of the Pipe Bundle. The five policemen who took the Bundle from Elk Head were ordered to return it. On the way back to the agency after depositing the sacred relic with its keeper, a cloud of mist, much like the one that appeared with the coming of the White Buffalo Calf Maiden, was seen. When it lifted, one of the policemen was dead. This happened twice more during the next few days until all five of the Indian policemen were dead."30.

The Indian Police had a large influence on the downfall of the Sioux and other Native Americans. It was said they came to offer themselves as proxies for the white man. On the reservations they enforced the laws and treated themselves to other liberties. Wallace Black Elk mentioned that they had not mellowed- out even in the twentieth century. "The really tough part was that it was our own people who were tracking us down [Wallace Black Elk and his grandparents]. They were Indian people. They wore uniforms and badges and carried clubs and guns. There were no roads so they would ride over there on horseback. When they came they would tear up our sacred stone-people-lodge – break it up and throw it into the fire. If they found one of our sacred bundles, they'd tear that up and throw it into the fire. If they found a Chanunpa, they would just smash that stone into a million pieces and throw the stem into the fire."31.

There were among several Sioux divisions many recognized Akicitas, whose responsibility as rotating police was to maintain order during camp movements and communal buffalo hunts. The Akicitas were a fraternal group, open to all able bodied young men and were rotated each season. The Akicitas as inseparable from the mainstream, enjoyed a high status in contrast to the tribal police, considered the white man's satrap by almost everyone.

At the same time as Ramakrishna and Vivekananda in nineteenth century India, generally the educated and middle classes turned their backs on India's heritage; Hinduism was ridiculed and these sepoys adapted European dress and mannerisms. Vivekananda berated these Westernized Indians. "Alas, to such a state is our country reduced! The people will look upon their own gold as brass, while the brass of the foreigner is gold to them."32.

Meditation, Prayer and Visions

In Vedanta, the persistent practice of a person's sadhana, imparted by one's guru, will, it is said, eventually lead the aspirant toward the withdrawal of his or her senses from external objects so that the focus is inward toward the Self. This is the goal of meditation, a practice connected to Raja Yoga. After years of unwavering practice, the practioner gradually attains an unbroken communication and awareness with his or her ishadevata (chosen ideal, a Christ or Buddha or any saint of any religion) within – thus succeeding to a higher state of consciousness, and a transformation of character.

Ramakrishna compares this level of accomplishment to a jug filled with water. When the jug is empty one hears the sound of water being poured, but when completely filled all sound ceases. Control of the senses deepens the aspirant's capacity for meditation; otherwise it is merely mechanical.

Meditation is part and parcel of Native American religious practice, but it differs somewhat among different cultures and schools of thought. For almost every person involved with this undertaking the importance of silence is always stressed. Ohiyesa declares that the Great Mystery is worshipped in silence and in solitude, and the contemplation is free from self-seeking. The silence implies that no speech is necessary in that it would be feeble and imperfect. "Therefore, the souls of my ancestors ascended to God in wordless adoration. It was solitary, because they believed that He is nearer to us in solitude, and there were no priests authorized to come between a man and his maker. None might exhort or confess or in any way meddle with the religious experience of another."[1].

The elderly Dakota warrior at the terminus of his life finds an affinity with an anemone flower blooming in the spring prairie. This is part of the ceremony of the Fourth Hill which represents old age. For every stage of life – infancy, youth, maturity, and old age – there is a corresponding ritual to reflect the outlook among the Dakota Sioux. The senor males seek out the flower with bare feet and tobacco. When the elder finds a blossom, he sits beside it, takes his pipe and salutes the Four Quarters of the earth, offering smoke to the blossom. As he smokes he meditates on the course of his lifetime: the joy of those who hailed his birth: "A man lies here!" When the tobacco has been consumed, he empties the ash from his pipe near the plant. Finally after plucking the flower, he returns to his lodge, singing the song of the pasque blossom which tells of the virtues of endurance and faithfulness to the end.

Wounye Waste Win, a Lakota declares, "I was told by an interpreter, 'As long as you pray from the heart, all the pipes that have ever been will back you if you have the honesty to pray for real from the heart, you will be heard.'"

The petitioner is coming directly in contact with his or her godhead or higher Self. In the context of both meditation and prayer, the Santee Sioux believe in two minds: the spiritual mind of the psyche and the physical mind of the ego. Through the application of prayer requiring fasting and other austerities, the individual is advised not to petition for favors of a personal or material nature, or anything relegated to the lower plane of the senses. Anything involved with ceremonies, charms, or incantations where selfish reward is sought, is seen by the Santee as stemming from the ego or physical self. Twylah Nitsch's attitude is similar to Ohiyesas'. "Whenever I see or hear a prayer written by an Indian that says, 'Great Spirit grant me this or that' – a prayer of supplication – I know that it has been infiltrated with other philosophies. A traditional Indian never asks, never offers prayers of supplication, he only offers prayers of thanks. This is a true, hard fact, and one that is important to an understanding of medicine."2.

Paula Allen, Grandmother of the Light, maintains that material objects are bestowed to the sincere spiritual seeker, but are not an automatic consequence of spiritual practice. "Tribal people, pagans, do not center their lives on belongings, so economic considerations are not of primary concern for them. They believe that our physical needs are taken care of as a consequence of our meeting our spiritual obligations, and fulfilling those obligations depends on our harmony with the universe."3.

For Native Americans material goods represent usage, especially those associated with sacredness. Sacred objects, rather than those leading to community status, are located in the world of meaning. They express prayer in a multitude of forms: symbolic designs are woven into fabrics, in the marking of beadwork, on pottery, and are expressed in sacred dances, rituals and songs.

THE SIX GRANDFATHERS: NICK BLACK ELK'S VISION

For most of us, sadhana takes many years of hard practice, before anything worth obtaining takes place. But for some people it is acquired instantaneously without austerities or serious effort: examples are St. Francis of Assisi, and St. Catherine of Genoa. Nick Black Elk obtained his epiphany through serendipity as a child of nine years, as he was overcome with a serious fever. The vision of the Six Grandfathers was revealed to the Oglala boy in the family tipi. Black Elk's experience would seem rather arcane to the modern Western mind, even the version as transcribed by John Neihardt in the 1930s when Black Elk was 69, still vigorous, his mind clear and functioning well. Black Elk had been sick 12 days, appearing like dead all the while, and Whirlwind Chase, Standing Bear's uncle, a medicine man, cured him.

Black Elk's vision was authentic, not a dream brought on by his feverish condition. Lame Deer explains the difference. "If you dream, that's no vision. Anybody can dream. And if you take an herb – well even the butcher boy at his meat counter will have a vision after eating peyote. The real vision has to come out of your own juices. It is not a dream; it is very real. It hits you sharp and clear like an electric shock. You are wide awake and suddenly, there is a person standing next to you who you know can't be there at all. Or somebody is sitting close by and all at once you see him also up on a hill a mile away. Yet you are not dreaming; your eyes are open. You have to work for this, empty your mind for it."4.

"Once you have experienced the real thing, you will never be satisfied with anything else. It will be all or nothing for you then."5.

St. Pierre and Tilda Long Soldier believe that any dream that lingers upon waking is worth considering, pondering over, because to the Lakota that dream is a means of the most essential communication – that with the spirit world. In the Lakota view, dreams are at times warnings of impending danger or life-style alterations or communication with a departed loved one.

Black Elk's vision was largely symbolic – animals and humans possessed protean interchangeability; as has been noted, among many Native Americans, the animal kingdom is traditionally accepted as relatives and brothers possessing souls and intelligence.

The key players in Black Elk's drama were herds of the most beautiful and exquisite horses imaginable, and the uncanny ancestors, the Six Grandfathers, held in high esteem and respect by all Sioux bands – the Six Powers of the universe. Both the horse and the eagle were held in the highest stature. The horse was immediately accepted as soon as it made its appearance on the plains. According to Lakota legend, the first horse made it appearance in the lives of the Indians already domesticated, contentedly munching the wild grass amidst the tipis. When the wild horses entered the Oglala's life, the Indians pursued the wild herds for the purpose, not only for the animal's usefulness, but for its worth as a trusted companion. The horse was tamed, and adorned with the most exquisite jewels, covered with sturdy saddle blankets comprised of the finest specimen of buffalo-skin robes; it was included in Lakota ceremonies, songs and dances, which were often dedicated to the horse, and it proved a compatible creature as it joined the warriors in the dances around the campfire.

Black Elk's vision was a kind of initiation for the nine-year-old boy, who would one day receive the full powers of the Six Grandfathers, the Oglala's holy ancestors. Black Elk's vision included a mythical world of a tipi built of cloud with a flaming rainbow door and, inside the Six Grandfathers were seated, and "they looked older than men could ever be – old like hills, like stars," and "also there was myself upon my bay before the tepee."

"Take courage, younger brother," the second Grandfather told Black Elk, "on earth a nation you shall make live for yours shall be the power of the white giant's wing, the cleansing wind."6.

Then the first Grandfather pointed to himself and said, "Look close at him who is your spirit now, for you are his body and his name is Eagle Wing Stretches. [Eagles are seen as important messengers between humankind and the sacred mystery – eagles carry the petitioner's prayers to the Great Spirit – partly because they can soar into the pure, rarefied air where the sacred can communicate with them above the polluting influence of earth], and saying this, he got up very tall and started running toward where the sun goes down; and suddenly he was a black horse that stopped and turned and looked at me, and the horse was very poor and sick; his ribs stood out."7.

SONG OF THE GREAT BLACK STALLION

In his vision, Black Elk sojourns included intervals

where his people lived peaceably and in harmony with all living things. The Song of the Great Black Stallion reached everywhere, "and it was more beautiful than anything can be. It was so beautiful that nothing anywhere could keep from dancing. The virgins danced, and all the circled horses. The leaves on the trees, the grasses on the hills and in the valleys, the waters in the creeks, and in the rivers and the lakes, the four-legged and the two legged, and the wings of the air – all danced together to the music of the stallion's song.

"And a voice said: 'All over the universe they have finished a day of happiness.' And looking down I saw that the whole wide circle of the day was beautiful and green, with all fruits growing and all things kind and happy."8. Black Elk was unspecific about the place and location of this pristine land. Perhaps it was the fabled hegira subscribed to by many Native Americans before the destructive advent of the white man; the good books of every major religion make room for such a place, e.g., the Garden of Eden.

Following Black Elk's vision of the "day of happiness", he received a premonition of the demise of the whole Sioux nation. "And the voice said: 'behold your nation, and remember what your Six Grandfathers gave you, for thenceforth your people will walk in difficulties...'9. "Then the people," continues Black Elk, "broke camp again, and I saw the black road before them towards where the sun goes down, and black clouds coming yonder, and they did not want to go but could not stay. And as they walked the third ascent...all the animals and fowls that were the people ran here and there...and all over the universe I could hear the winds at war like wild beasts fighting.

"Then when the people were getting ready to begin the fourth ascent, the Voice spoke like some one weeping, and it said: 'Look there upon your nation.' And when I looked down, the people were all changed back to human, and they were thin, their faces sharp, for they were starving. Their ponies were only hide and bones, and their holy tree [the Flowering Tree] was gone."10.

This was fact in the case of the great warrior, Crazy Horse, and the Cheyenne chief, Dull Knife, who in the wake of these harsh conditions, one year after their victory at the Little Big Horn, surrendered at Fort Robinson. Sitting Bull was lured out of his Canadian sanctuary by the generous promises of white calvry officers, never fulfilled. Members of their own tribe betrayed both Oglala notables: Crazy Horse and Sitting Bull were assassinated with the complicity of the Indian police – old comrades in-arms, who shared the glory over the Seventh Calvry not long before. Black Elk continues, "I was all alone on a broad plain now with my feet upon the earth, alone but for the spotted eagle guarding me. I could see my people's village far ahead, and I walked very fast, for I was homesick now. Then I saw my own tepee and inside I saw my mother and my father bending over a sick boy that was myself. And as I entered the tepee, someone was saying: 'The boy is coming to; you had better give him some water.'

"Then I was sitting up; and I was sad because my mother and my father didn't seem to know I had been so far away."11.

Ramakrishna answers Black Elk's doubting-Thomas's, who might dismiss his experience out-of-hand as hallucinatory, brought about by his high fervor, in regards to a disciple's dream about Chaitaniya, a fifteenth century Indian saint.

Disciple: "But sir, it was only a dream."

Ramakrishna: "Is a dream a small thing?" "The Master's voice was choked. His eyes were filled with tears. Sri Ramakrishna was told of a devotee who had divine visions even while he --was awake. The Master said: 'I am not surprised. Narendra [Vivekananda] too sees forms of God nowdays.'"12.

Black Elk was sure that he was then too young to understand his vision, he only felt it. "It was the pictures I remembered and the words that went with them; for nothing I have ever seen with my eyes was so clear and bright as what my vision showed me; and no words that I have ever heard with my ears were like the words I heard. I did not have to remember these things; they have remembered themselves all these years. It was as I grew older that the meanings came clearer and clearer out of the picture, and the words; and even now I know that more was shown to me than I can tell."13.

Lame Deer believes that every individual has a spiritual guide within, and that is how spiritual communion is enacted from within. "We Sioux believe that there is something within us that controls us, something like a second person almost. We call it Nagi, what other people might call soul, spirit or essence. One can't see it, feel it or taste it, but that time on the hill - and only that once - I knew it was there inside me. Then I felt the power surge through me like a flood. I cannot describe it, but it filled all of me. Now I knew for sure that I would become a Wicasa Wakan, a medicine man. Again, I wept, this time with happiness."14.

The Sioux after life is populated with benevolent and malevolent spirits. In the Indians' view each person has a spirit guide inherited or assigned at birth. It remains within him or her for the duration of their lives like the Christian guardian angel. The Nagi is not integral to the individual but independent. The Nagi accompanies the subtle body or spirit (some call it the soul) to different lokas or spheres according to the person's karma. According to Wallace Black Elk, its mission is primarily to offer "health" and "help."

Swami Vivekananda agrees, he discloses the Vedic version

of the Sioux Nagi. "The Vedantist says, the cause of all that is apparently evil is the limitation of the unlimited. The love which gets limited into little channels and seems to be evil eventually comes out at the other end and manifests itself as God. The Vedanta also says that the cause of all this apparent evil is in ourselves. Do not blame any supernatural being, neither be hopeless and despondent, nor think we are in a place from which we can never escape unless someone comes and lends us a helping hand. That cannot be, says the Vedanta. We are like silkworms; we make the thread out of our own substance and spin the cocoon, and in course of time are imprisoned inside. But this is not forever. In that cocoon we shall develop spiritual realization, and like the butterfly come out free. This network of Karma we have woven around ourselves and in our ignorance we feel as if we are bound, and weep and wail for help. But help does not come from without; it comes from within ourselves. Cry to all the gods in the universe. I cried for years, and in the end I found that I was helped. But help came from within. And I had to undo what I had done by mistake. That is the only way I had to cut the net which I had thrown around myself and the power to do this is within."15.

Every Step is a Walking Prayer: The Sweat Lodge

Wallace Black Elk learned at the feet of tribal elders about the sacredness of the "Stone Lodge" or sweat lodge. In the Lakota language Tunkan Tipi: Tun means "birth", Kan means "age." The word tipi means "Windbreaker" or "shelter."1.

In the truest spirit of simplicity the penitent or "Quester" in his journey to the lodge is undergoing a sadhana. "So every step you take [on the walk to the lodge] is a prayer," says Black Elk, "the old people told us this. So every step you take is a prayer. But it seems like some people are in the wrong step. If you take a wrong step, then you are in the wrong all your life. If you take a right step, then you'll be in the right the rest of your life. So the right step is from this lodge. So whenever you stop, always stop at this lodge...so it's a place to be purified. When you pray for people, you have to wipe yourself on the last round. Then all the contamination will go away. Whatever your intentions are, the spirits will add more power, more strength to it...Good words and good thoughts will come out. Then you think something good, and you do something good. So they return to you with that power built inside you."2.

For a description of the sweat lodge and the subsequent preparations for the purification ritual, we shall start with Michael Steltenkamp, a non-Indian Jesuit priest and Lakota confidant. "The pit was dug directly in front of the sweat lodge door – an old buffalo skull with a broken horn staring coldly at the entrance."3. Lame Deer elaborates describing the pit as a circle within a circle, which forms the hut. "A circle within a circle stands for life, for which has no end. Plants, animals, men are born and die, but the Indian people will live."4. Lame Deer calls this lodge the Lakota tabernacle.

Sacred material is gathered for the inipi or purification ceremony. Rocks are gathered from the prairie and hills; firewood is collected, but ideally only cottonwood, the Lakota's most sacred tree is used, however, sometimes substitutes are approved when cottonwood is unavailable. At the side of a creek white willow trees are cut down and cut up into sticks: two by fours and two by sixes resembling laths capable of bending easily; they are planted in a circle like a beehive – tied together they fit this shape. The sticks form a square on top which represents the universe and the four cardinal directions. The willow wands form the skeleton of the sweat lodge hut. Lame Deer compares them to the bones of the Oglala people, but covered up – sometimes with buffalo hides or skins of other animals.

The Lakota believe that the animus of all living things is inside the hut. The earth is the Siouan grandmother; all life emanates from the Divine Mother.

In the center of the hut a hole is scooped out for the altar, which will hold boiling hot stones. The scooped out earth is salvaged to form a ridge for the spirits to traverse, ten steps away from the sweat lodge. The final step contains a small mound – symbolic of Unci – the grandmother to which the penitents express their thanks for what the earth means to them.

The center pit or altar signifies Wakicagapi, a beloved, departed relative, who can be recalled to earth during the hot altar ceremony. Father Steltenkamp supplies his own experience. "The lodge's real hot 'altar' is said to represent the power of Wakan Tanka, as, indeed the four elements of air, earth, fire, and water combine to produce an intense feeling of naked energy. Aliveness was inescapably felt as throbbing flesh pounded the fact of existence, and fragrant sage suggests its divine authorship."5.

The ceremonial leader enters the hut through the entrance facing west with his pipe; he covers the ground with sage, the Lakota's sacred plant symbolizing the spirit of trees and plants that accompany the penitent(s) inside. The leader burns sweet grass and the aroma covers every part of the lodge, thus, everything is sacred, and negative thoughts and attitudes are driven away, And the penitents, says Lame Deer are symbolically going to experience rebirth, "like a baby coming out of your mother's womb, our real mother, the earth."

Leonard Crow Dog accounts his own experience – his feelings inside the Grandmother's womb. "Inside we were huddling in total darkness. All I could see was a red glow from the heated stones. I could feel their warmth. Now I knew that I was truly in Grandmother's womb, in the darkness of the womb, the darkness of the soul. In the warmth and moisture, I felt that this was myself before being born."6.

The heated rocks, a major part of the inipi (inipi means to live again) are brought in by a forked stick, or any handy device – sometimes deer antlers – and the penitents say "Pilamaye" – thanks. Rocks are placed to represent the grandmother earth and the four directions for the sky and the grandfather spirit. Extra stones may be placed according to the kind of ceremony conducted.

The pipe is lit and passed around – symbolizing as a link to all participants as brothers, who rub the smoke, the vapor of the heated rocks all around their bodies as they pray to the Great Spirit, and all the sacred rocks linked to the Great Spirit through the Great Mystery – Everything is God. The rocks have no physical orifices, "but they exhale the breath of life." The hut is now completely enclosed in darkness. Water is sprinkled over the red-hot rocks – the water is ice cold, "So here is a unifying," says Lame Deer, "the earth and the sky, the water of life and the sacred breath of the spirit, grandfather and grandmother coming together. There is a great surge of power. You inhale that breath, drink in the water, the white steam. It represents clouds, the living soul, life."7.

Many "mainstreamed" Lakota have returned to the "Indian Way". Red Dawn Wolf is such a "Rainbow Man" and he relates his experience of a contemporary Inipi. "The inipi lodge is the womb of Mother Earth. In the darkness underneath the canopy of bent saplings with tarps placed over them, sitting on the ground, smelling her musty smell, you are close to her. We put a sprinkle of sage and sweetgrass on the hot rocks as each was placed in the round pit in the middle of the lodge. The sweet smoke rose up to erase the negative thoughts that so easily linger in our minds and to help set our hearts into the receptive condition needed for this sacred ceremony. The rocks are greeted as old friends who have come to help. These rocks held a specialness in that they had been so dearly sought and seemed to have been specially placed for our use. The flap was closed and the first of four 'endurances' began. Each phase centers on a direction, usually starting in either the east or the west 'depending on the purpose of the ceremony'. We started this ceremony in the west. We called on the spirit guides to help us, and I heard loving prayers from my friends asking those helpers to aid me on my quest. More drumming and the flap was opened. The process was repeated for each direction; water was thrown on the rocks and they sizzled their reply. A sweat must be experienced again and again to be fully appreciated and understood. It is clear that if approached in humble openness, the ceremony is far more than just a 'sauna' with sweat running off one's body."8.

Lame Deer concludes that the power of the stones and the vaporous heat, "heals you. That steam stops at the skin, but that earth-power penetrates your body and mind. It cures many sicknesses – arthritis, rheumatism. It heals the wounds of your mind. This inipi is our little church. It is not like some white churches where people sit in pews, showing off their fine clothes. The inipi is different. There is no bragging and no impurity here. Just naked humans, huddling in the dark, close to the earth and to the spirit. If the spirit is with you, you could pick up the glowing rock and it would not hurt you."9.

There is a structural relationship between the sweat lodge and the hanbelachia or Vision Quest. A sweat lodge or inipi may be experienced independent of any other ritual, for both spiritual and salutary purposes, the inipi serves as a preparatory and concluding ceremony for the Vision Quest. In contrasting both, the sweat lodge can be an independent ritual, whereas the hanbelachia is partially dependant on the sweat lodge for maximum efficacy.

HANBELACHIA, THE VISION QUEST

In the Vision ritual of the Oglala, the warrior sees that humankind's relationship to all things is Brahman or the Great Spirit. The realization of this sublime spiritual truth can be manifest through the "Crying for a Vision" [viz. Hanbelachia] ritual. The lamenter in his vision may receive a messenger in an animal form. Perhaps a spotted eagle may come to him from the west, or a black eagle from the east, or even the redheaded woodpecker from the south. This helps the lamenter to understand that all created beings are sacred. Everything has a wochangi or influence to further the devotee's understanding or knowledge. The animals and birds and other entities are "reflections" in a material form of the divinity; attachment to the form is for the sake of the principle contained in the form.

Power comes to the man and sometimes a woman in dreams and visions. Once it is obtained, it is said to be character transforming. Black Horse's hanbelachia is as follows: when Black Horse left the sweat lodge, he was no longer a penitent, since he had been purified by the rigors of the inipi. At the hanbelachia or vision hill, Black Horse was acknowledged as a "dreamer", which accrued to it much status and influence. Visions are differentiated from ordinary dreams because visions come only when the individual is fully awake. As a profession, the dreamer status does not bring the practitioner material gain, but there are unquestionable advantages and honorarium that augments the dreamer's economic well being. Power comes to an individual in dreams and visions. Once it is achieved it becomes inherent in a dreamer's physical and mental make up. Based on the proclivities of animals, it is limited to those specific areas of achievement. For instance, if an eagle brings the vision, the dreamer will inherit its keen sense of intelligence – its agile powers. Moreover, as a trust, it carries grave responsibilities. But its advantages outweigh its disadvantages, and due to the fact that prestige and presumed security are so universally recognized that most Sioux males take special pains to obtain it. It must be noted at the outset that not all Vision Quests bring about visions.

When Black Horse dreamed of thunder, he naturally associated it with the Heyoka (clown) clan, but he hesitated acknowledging the downside of this fraternity: endurance of harsh austerities and isolation from tribal communion. Writes William Powers, "The Thunder Beings' voices diminish to a murmur. Their eyes close, sucking up what is left of the lightning. Hooded giants on parti-colored horses drive their slaves homeward to the hills in the west, firmly holding their leashes of lightning. The gods have made their presence known so the people may understand that human arrogance is not permitted – that men are antlike figures humbly crawling across the universe, no more and no less important than the other creatures of the world."10.

Vivekananda welcomes the admonishment of the Thunder Beings. "We are absolutely one; we are physically one, we are mentally one, and as spirit, it goes without saying, that we are one, if we believe in spirit at all. This oneness is the one fact that is being proved everyday by modern science. To proud man it is told: You are the same as that little worm there; think not that you are something enormously different from it…You have been that in a previous incarnation, and the worm has crawled up to this man state, of which you are so proud. This grand preaching, the oneness of things, making us one with everything that exists, is the great lesson to learn, for most of us are very glad to be made one with higher beings, but nobody wants to be made one with lower beings."11.

Apprehensive about the downside of his dream, Black Horse paid a visit to the renown mystic,

Horn Chips, known to have been Crazy Horse's spiritual guide. Comments Powers, "No one to my knowledge, and this is verified in the Yuwipi literature, has been associated so dramatically with early forms of ritual curing as Horn Chips."12.

When Horn Chips was confident that Black Horse's intention of undergoing the rigors of the hanbelachia was sincere, the shaman, himself, a Heyoka agreed to be his sponsor, knowing that Black Horse came from a family of successful dreamers.

Trekking along sacred grounds, Black Horse beside Horn Chips was accompanied by four other Heyokas, who would share the inipi ceremony with its hundred boiling rocks.

At daybreak, Horn Chips gave Black Horse a piece of pemmican and a sip of water, and then the party of six men proceeded to the Eagle Nest Butte, the site of the Vision Quest. William Powers describes such a location. "When you reach the top you are struck by the wholeness of nature. You can see far in every direction, and you realize how much more you know about the world than people down below. Then you are overcome by the price you pay for this knowledge. You are alone."13.

After affixing the site with the proscribed Wakan articles: tobacco sticks and colored banners, pitched at the four corners, signifying the four directions, the supplicant, in order to propitiate the spirits who hovered around the perimeter enclosing the pit, offered pieces of his flesh severed from his forearm and thighs, tied together in a bundle, attached to the tobacco sticks. Each color of the cloth banners symbolizes a direction: west, black (mysterious spirit of the west), north, red, east, yellow (healing), south, white. The significance of these flags will cause the sacred stones existing at the four quarters of the universe to fly to the meeting place. The tobacco offerings represent all living species that associate with humankind.

When Horn Chips deemed the preparations satisfactory, the shaman left with the other Heyokas, and the ephebe was all alone, standing naked and holding the stem to his consecrated pipe, as he raised it toward the first rays of the sun. When dusk arrived Black Horse faced the west, raising the pipe stem toward the setting sun.

Black Horse spent his first sleepless night lying in the pit on a bed of sage. Just before dawn, his first arcane response arrived in the form of an unseen voice. The Dreamer was informed that his sadhana would be so rigorous that few men had undergone the challenge completely. "The Thunder Dream came to you so that you would undertake this." The invisible voices occupied Black Horse's first day, and he saw an eagle, which told him his test would soon begin.

A series of visions followed, and the confused novice entered an ethereal plane: Black Horse saw his son, Bad Hand shot to death in a quarrel, and brought back to life again at the command of a spirit. Subsequently, the invisible became manifest in animal forms: a prairie hawk told him to be patient and flew away.

Hungry and desiccated, Black Horse, "walked away crying and all nature was talking."14. Voices called to him, "Your grandfathers are returning."

Black Horse experienced strange episodes. In the darkness, he was able only to make out a single object: a swaying tipi with a hole on top from which mysterious voices were heard. The stentorian voices were louder than a screeching owl's. As in Nick Black Elk's childhood vision, a group of grandfathers appeared – seven of them. A wizen man seated to the north informed Black Horse that he was in the company of seven grandfathers few people had ever seen. The Dreamer studied these grotesques forms: miniature elders, covered with fur, sunflower-shaped eyes and horns above their ears. In the minds of the Advaitic non-dual Vedantins and Lakota, these sagacious oddities were not seen as caricatures of Satan; quite the contrary: if God is not everything, but everything is God, the seven grandfathers were, therefore, emanations of the Great Spirit. In the relative world of maya, Brahman/Great Spirit is manifested through infinite names and forms, mired in contradiction or pairs of opposites. Thus, as a cycle of creation unfolds, beauty is only recognized when ugliness exists. In the realm of the absolute, the grandfathers are as beautiful as the White Buffalo Calf Woman – both inseparable in terms of the Great Mystery. Neither Vedantins nor the Sioux believe in the devil. God and the devil are one says Swamiji – one river flowing in opposite directions. Comments Eagle Man of the Rainbow people, "The white Missionaries tell us of a hell they have created. There is no evidence of hell (or a devil either) in nature; therefore, most traditionals do not swallow this belief of the white man. No Indians have yet seen a devil, and they wonder if white people truthfully have ever seen one." 15.

Vivekananda elaborates on the relative relationship between beauty and ugliness. "When there is real purification of the body, external and internal, there arises neglect of the body, and the idea of keeping it nice vanishes. A face which others call most beautiful will appear to the Yogi as merely animal, if there is not intelligence behind it. What the world calls a very common face he regards as heavenly, if the spirit shines behind it. This thirst after body is the great bane of human life. So the first sign of the establishment of purity is that you do not care to think you are a body."16.

A Grandfather holding a pipe told Black Horse, "Grandson, the birds and animals on earth will hear you when you ask anything of them. Now you are between the sky and the earth. Your grandfathers living between the earth and sky will help you in administering medicine to save life on earth. It is to your Grandfathers that you should appeal to help. No matter if you are calling from the depths of the earth, your voice will be heard and your appeal will be answered."17.

Furthermore, Black Horse got the message that his calling would be that of a medicine man, and he would be empowered to save the lives of many suffering people, but the gifts received in compensation should be rejected and immediately turned over to the worthy poor. When the Dreamer's encounter with the Grandfathers drew to a close, the last thing heard was an echo instructing him to be kind to all men and animals, his own family in particular. Soon the voices grew fainter, but Black Horse could make out the departing advice to never forget everything told to him and to remember everything he had seen and experienced.

Black Horse awoke to his normal consciousness at Eagle Nest Butte, his pipe still in his hands. At daybreak he met Horn Chips engaged in disassembling the ceremonial paraphernalia. "Horn Chip's family died when he was young. He went to live with his grandmother. The other children made so much fun of him that he decided to commit suicide. On his way to a lonely spot to end his life, he heard a voice that said it was that of the Great Spirit. The voice told Horn Chips not to kill himself, that he was destined to become a great man. Horn Chips was told to go to a high mountain, dig a hole four feet deep, cover it with boughs, and stay there four days with no food or drink. Horn Chips followed directions. When he was in the pit, he had a vision. A snake came to him from the Great Spirit and gave him his instructions."18. According to Powers the arrangement of the vision pit is identical with that of Black Horse's, and undoubtedly it was the high mountain of Eagle Nest Butte, where eagles were trapped in the pit, that Horn Chips was told to dig; modern Vision Quests may be based on Horn Chips' design.

Horn Chips and Black Horse left Eagle Nest Butte and stopped at the sweat lodge where other Heyokas were conducting an inipi. Horn Chips interpreted Black Horse's vision of the Grandfathers and indicated the proper herbs and Wotawe or sacred formulae used by practitioners of the healing arts. With this completed, Black Horse was told his vision was successful, and his sponsor initiated him into the Heyoka clan, which the Dreamer received with mixed feelings. True to the Thunder gods' promise, Black Horse had witnessed the shooting death of Bad Hand, his son at the hands of another tribal member, but the dead man was restored to life two days later.

Black Horse felt ambivalent about his initiation into the Heyoka. He compared the lot of a Heyoka to the rewarding responsibilities of other clans: the Buffalo, the Bear, the Wolf, and even the Elk and Deer. Those conferred on the Heyoka always fell short. His future was clouded with dread: saving lives without compensation, enduring the humiliating laughter of children, going about in the raiment of tattered rope, existing in a makeshift tipi. Only if he had a highly successful career would he receive the deference of his people.

Undoubtedly many skeptics would look upon the hanbelachia with derisive scorn, labeling the Indians' strange encounters as hallucinations stemming from the exertions of long fasting and exposure to the raw elements of heat and cold, not least the whimsical fantasies of naive shamans.

Many consumers of psychedelic drugs claim similar "visions", but when the substance wears off, the individual is left dumbfounded and sometimes physically impaired. Might it be pointed out that many Biblical and Eastern ascetics and luminaries underwent fasting and similar endurances before receiving such esoteric encounters and communion with God – Jesus, Buddha are the most notable who make up the list, as was Ramakrishna, who spent twelve years of hard austerities before the Divine Mother revealed herself to him.

As we have seen in the case of Satyakama, Vivekananda pointed out that every revelation an individual perceives is really an emanation from within. Therefore, Black Horse's vision was far from a figment of his imagination. When asked by a disciple about the fearful experiences an aspirant has prior to the attainment of realization – are these mental projections? – the Swami replied, "What else but that? The aspiring soul, of course, does not make out at that time that all these are external manifestations of his own mind. But all the same, there is nothing outside of it. Even what you see as this world does not exist outside. It is all mental projection. When the mind becomes functionless, it reflects the Brahman-consciousness. Then the vision of all spheres of existence may supervene 'whatsoever sphere one may call up in mind.' Whatsoever is resolved on becomes realized at once. He, who, even on attaining this state of unfalsified self-determination, preserves his watchfulness and is free from the bondage of desire, verily attains to the knowledge of Brahman. But he who loses his balance after reaching this state, gets the manifold powers but falls off from the supreme goal."19.

"When the Buddha was on the point of merging in Samadhi (superconsciousness), Mara [maya] made his appearance. There was really no Mara extraneous to the mind; it was only the external reflection of the mind's previous Samskaras."20.

Contrary to the reservations Black Horse felt upon receiving the news of his future being a clown, Horn Chips, the great Lakota rishi (seer) wore his Heyoka status as a badge of honor and enjoyed the respect of his people. Horn Chips was revered for his power, which included his ability to change the weather, to find lost objects, and to point out the location of missing persons. It was said that Horn Chips made his disciple Crazy Horse impervious to life-threatening wounds incurred on the battlefield.

Standing Bear identifies the marvelous powers attributed to Horn Chips. "Chips was another Stone Dreamer and his fame was wide among his people, for he would go into the sweat-bath and there locate lost articles or horses and absent people. While taking the purification ceremony the Tunkes or hot stones, brought great inspiration to Chips, so when he went to the place of vigil, they came to him in spirit and offered him services. So Chips always carried stones, some of them painted in colors, in his medicine bag. When he was making medicine they would fly to him, and they could be heard striking the tipi, and after we moved into houses I have heard them dropping down the chimney and have seen them lying about on the floor where they had fallen."21.

Lame Deer pays tribute to the contributions made by Horn Chips a century before. "Without him, maybe our religion would have died out. During the darkest years he kept his vision alive, worked it for the good of the people...If he hadn't taught us, there would be no medicine men left among us now."22.

Lakota Generosity

The Lakota lived in a community where the proverbial expression is succinctly told: One for all, and all for one. Ohiyesa speaks for the Sioux nation as a whole. "Public giving is part of every important ceremony. It properly belongs to the celebration of birth, marriage, death... whenever it is desired to do special honor to any person or event. Upon such occasions it is common to give to the point of utter impoverishment. The Indian in his simplicity literally gives away all that he has, to relatives, to guests of another tribe or clan, but above all to the poor and the aged, from whom he can hope for no return. Finally, the gift to the 'Great Mystery' the religious offering, may be of little value in itself, but to the giver's own thought it should carry the meaning and reward of true sacrifice."1.

Ernest Thompson Seton compiled a series of quotations on

Native American religious behavior entitled The Gospel of the Red Man. Seton cites Tom Newcomb, his guide in 1912 and 1914 in his excursion through Indian territory and his findings while almost universal among the native peoples, apply emphatically among the Lakota and other Sioux bands. "I tell you I never saw more kindness or real Christianity anywhere. The poor, the sick, the aged, the widows and the orphans were always looked after first. Whenever we moved camp, someone took care that the widow's lodges were moved first and set up first. After every hunt, a good-sized chunk of meat was dropped at each door where it was most needed. I was treated like a brother, and I tell you I have never seen any community of church people that was as truly Christian as that band of Indians."2.

The Lakota was taught to give copiously, especially charity to the elderly and infirmed. The Lakota child was taught to be generous for the sake of becoming brave and strong. The most charitable was the person who gives away his most cherished possessions. It was the custom to hold "Give-away dances" to distribute valuable gifts.

Lame Deer provides an example of an Oglala who carried the ideal of charity to its extremity. "I once heard of an Indian who lost a leg in an industrial accident. He got about fifthteen thousand dollars in insurance money. In no time his place was overrun with more than a hundred hungry relatives. They came in old jalopies, in buckboards, on horseback or on foot. From morning to night a pick-up truck was making round trips between his place and the nearest store, hauling beef and bread and crates of beer to keep all of those lean bellies full. In the end they brought a few scrub steers and did their own butchering. The fun lasted a few weeks; then the money was gone. A day after that the relatives were gone, too. That man had no regrets. He said he wished he'd lose his other leg so that he could start all over again. This man had become quite a hero, even to other tribes, and he was welcome everywhere."3.

"[The Lakota] also saw that the cows [female buffalo] readily adopt orphans and displayed generosity in allowing the starlings to nest in their wooly caps. These behaviors are thought to be closely tied to what is expected of humans."4.

Hoarding and self indulgence and possessions for mere prestige were inconceivable to the Lakota who accumulated on the basis of need. If a man was without a horse, the chief's responsibility was to see that he got one; if a tipi was needed, the members of his band acted collectively to secure one.

No tradition of merciless torture and killing was in the Lakota tradition. The Oglala was governed by chivalry in the rules of war. Examples have turned up that courageous captives were invited to tribal feasts, not as prisoners of war, but as guests of honor. Says Standing Bear, "When the game was over the 'guests' were dressed in the finery of the hosts, given the best horses in the band and allowed to go home in state."5.

Slavery in any form was disallowed by the Lakota. Not only did every person engage in his or her dutiful task, but even animals were allowed to roam freely. Animals and Indians, as we have seen ample examples, were natural allies, learning from each other and bonded in friendship. Sitting Bull had abolished slavery in the Hunkpapa band and told his people either to adopt captives or set them free.

Warfare was regarded as an institute of the Great Mystery, and it was engaged in like a medieval tournament of tribal display, courage and skill with elaborate rules. It was never intended for territorial aggrandizement. Ohiyesa remarks, "It was common in early times for a battle or skirmish to last all day, with great display of daring and horsemanship, but with scarcely more killed and wounded than may be carried from the field during a university game of football."6. Only with the arrival of the white man did the Indian extend his intentions to pilfer horses from enemy tribes, which became standard practice and was not considered dishonorable. With the white man came liquor and lethal weapons, and there was a lapse in chivalrous codes. With the introduction of breech-loading repeating rifles made the Sioux warrior the world's most renowned cavalryman.

Lame Deer describes a Lakota tableau without jails, without locks and keys because, "Before our white brothers came to civilize us we had no jails. Therefore we had no criminals. You can't have criminals without a jail. We had no locks or keys, and so we had no thieves. If a man was so poor that he had no horse, tipi or blanket, someone gave him these things. We were too uncivilized to set much value on personal belongings. We wanted to have things only in order to give them away. We had no money, and therefore a man's worth couldn't be measured by it. We had no written law, no attorneys or politicians, therefore we couldn't cheat. We really were in a bad way before the white man came, and I don't know how we managed to get along without the basic things which, we are told, are absolutely necessary to a civilized society."7.

THE GAY COMMUNITY

Neither scorned nor ostracized, nor ridiculed, or worse, the Lakota found a place for gay men and women, and accommodated their sometimes unique talents into the fold. In the Lakota language gay people were called winktes and enjoyed a modicum of status and prestige.

There was a consensus among the Lakota that the winktes

followed a unique lifestyle on the instructions received in visions usually from Anukite' or "Double Woman", even from women in their period of menstruation. In a typical vision, the dreamer could chose between a burden strap or an arrow. The burden strap signified the woman's role, the arrow, the masculine.

According to William Powers, "Winktes were indeed considered the most sacred and played important roles in Lakota culture. They frequently did (and do) take care of the old and feeble and orphaned children. Although it is claimed that men chose the Winkte role to avoid danger; Winktes in fact often went on war parties. Winktes were also regarded as good hunters, although they usually hunted alone for small game and did not participate in the larger communal buffalo hunts. One psychiatrist explained the herdache [French corruption of Arabic word bardaj meaning slave] as an institution that permitted some to cross dress to prevent unsuspecting heterosexuals from being 'recruited' as homosexuals, but this is clearly a twentieth century idea unsupported in Lakota ideology."8.

Since the true transvestite was accorded his sanction through receiving his instruction in a dream, the winkte was recognized as Wakan. He might have certain powers of healing like a shaman; one numinous prerogative was the right to bestow private or secret names to children.

Blue Whirlwind comments, "There is a belief that if a winkte is asked to name a child, the child will grow up without sickness. My grandson was given the name Iron Horse when he was three days old by a winkte, and I gave him a horse.

"Fathers will go to the winkte and flirt with him. Whatever the winkte says will become the secret name, and this he will name the child. Winkte names are often unmentionable and, therefore, are not often used. Girls never had winkte names."9.

The introduction of a winkte, in the naming of a child ceremony was assurance of a long life for the child; usually a horse was given as a form of compensation. On the other hand, winkte names were rarely used because they had a pornographic connotation. A winkte was supposed to live a long life.

Lame Deer further elaborates on this notion. "Winktes were men who dressed like women, looked like women and acted like women. They did so by their own choice or in obedience to a dream. They were not like other men, but the Great Spirit made them winktes and we accepted them as such. They were supposed to have the gift of prophecy, and the secret name a winkte gave to a child was believed to be especially powerful and effective. In former days a father gave to a winkte a fine horse in return for such a name."10.

Ramakrishna, too, touched upon the androgynous nature of humankind and the universe by making himself a living example of it. According to Swami Vivekananda, Ramakrishna taught that the idea of sex was illusionary. "Then came to him [Ramakrishna] the conviction that to be perfect, the idea of sex must go, because the soul has no sex, the soul is neither male nor female. It is only in the body that sex exists, and the man who desires to reach the Spirit cannot at the same time hold to sex distinctions. Having been born in a masculine body, [he] wanted to bring the feminine idea into everything. He began to think that he was a woman, spoke like a woman, behaved like a woman, and lived as a member of the household among the women of a good family, until after months of this discipline his mind became changed and he entirely forgot the idea of sex. Thus his whole view of life became changed."11.

Back to the Blanket Intolerance

After the Sioux bands were subdued by the superior numbers and weaponry of many cavalry divisions, sent in pursuit of the Indian to conquer him and force him on to the reservations, the subjugated nations, not only had to suffer the indignation of corrupt white agents, sent by the Bureau of Indian Affairs, but the Christian missionaries encamped and castigated the red man for his "pagan" beliefs and drove all sacred practices underground. Sitting Bull's prophetic warnings of the white man's retaliation for the Indians' victory at Little Big Horn came down with a vengeance in the duration of a single year.

At first there was a fierce protest. Walking Buffalo of the Sioux led the outcry in Tatana Mani (Walking Buffalo of the Stonies): "When we sang our praises to the sun or moon or wind, you said we were worshiping idols. Without understanding, you condemned us as lost souls just because our form of worship was different from yours. We saw the Great Spirit's work in almost everything: sun, moon, trees, wind, and mountains. Sometimes we approached him through these things. Was that so bad? I think we have a true belief in the supreme being, a stronger faith than that of most whites who have called us pagans."1.

Nick Black Elk suffered the bigotry at the hands of a Jesuit priest during his second healing as a medicine man in 1904. Lucy Looks Twice, Black Elk's daughter, comments, "In 1904 my father was called upon to doctor a little boy in Payabaya – seven miles north of Holy Rosary Mission. The boy's family wanted my father to doctor their son because they heard he was good at it. So my father walked over there carrying his medicine and everything he needed for the ceremony.

"When he got there, he found the sick boy lying in a tent. So right away he prepared to doctor him. My father took his shirt off, put tobacco offerings in the sacred place, and started pounding on his drum. He called on the spirits to heal the boy in a very strong action. Dogs were there and they were barking [seeing the spirits]. My father was really singing away, beating his drum and using his rattle when along came one of the Blackrobes – Father Lindebrner [as we called him], Ate' Petecela [translated as Little Father]. At that time, the priests usually traveled by team and buggy throughout the reservations. That's what Ate' Petecela was driving.

"So he went into the tent and saw what my father was doing. Father Lindebner had already baptized the boy and had come to give him the last rites anyway, he took whatever my father had prepared on the ground and threw it all into the stove. He took the drum and rattle and threw them outside the tent. Then he took my father by the neck and said, 'Satan, get out!'"2.

Swami Vivekananda had a Father Lindebrner in mind when he commented on Ghantakarna, an unconscionable fanatic. "The story is told of a devotee by the name of Ghantakarna, the bell-eared, who was so fanatical a worshipper of Siva that he did not wish even to hear the name of any other deity; so he wore two bells tied to his ears in order to drown the sound of any voice uttering other divine names. At the sight of his intense devotion, Siva wanted to teach him that there was no difference between Himself and Vishnu; so He appeared before him as half Vishnu and half Siva. At that moment the devotee was waving incense before Him; but so great was the bigotry of Ghantakarna that when he saw the fragrance of the incense entering the nostril of Vishnu, he thrust his finger into it to prevent the Deity from enjoying the sweet smell."3.

Standing Bear comments on the effect of the clash of civilizations had on the Indian's psyche. "And it was the very beneficence of the Indian's attitude toward his own religion that left him unprepared for the harshness of the white man's vindictive religion. He was mystified, baffled, and bewildered by it and its infliction upon him, in some cases, of unspeakable cruelty."4.

Lame Deer describes how the intolerance of the missionaries affected him. "In 1920 they wouldn't even allow us to be dead in our own way. We had to be buried in the Christian fashion. It was as if they wanted to take my mother to a white boarding school way up there. For four days I felt my mother's nagi, her presence, her soul near me. I felt that some of her goodness was staying with me. The priest talked about eternity. I told him we Indians did not believe in a forever and forever. We say that only the rocks and the mountains last, but even they will disappear. There's a new day coming, but no forever, I told him, 'When my time comes, I want to go where my ancestors have gone.' The priest said, 'That may be hell.' I told him that I'd rather be frying with a Sioux grandmother or uncle than sit on a cloud playing a harp with a pale-faced stranger."5.

Few Indians, not least the Lakota, will ever forget the holocaust at Wounded Knee when the Lakota attempted to dance the Ghost Dance in desperation. The Ghost Dance took place on the Pine Ridge reservation in 1890. The central character that made this happen was a Paiute Indian, Wovoka, said to be a prophet. In 1889 Wovoka was ill with fever during an eclipse of the sun. In tandem with Wovoka's experience, he entered the spirit world and was given sacred teachings.

When Wovoka returned to the Paiutes, he gave them the gist of his vision predicated on an optimistic prophecy: the earth would become a paradise after they danced the Ghost Dance for five days which he taught them. The people's depression turned to joyful enthusiasm; the gist of what he taught them was easily digested: the earth would be renewed; the Indian dead would return to life, all suffering and death would cease. In Lame Deer's words, "Eighty years ago our people danced until they dropped from exhaustion, swooning, fainting, seeing visions. They danced in this way to bring back their dead, to bring back the buffalo. A prophet had told them that through the power of the Ghost Dance the earth would roll up like a carpet, with all the white man's works – the fences and the mining towns with their whorehouses, the factories and the farms with their stinking, unnatural animals, the railroads and the telegraph poles, the whole works. And underneath this rolled-up white man's world we would find again the flowering prairie, unspoiled with its herds of buffalo and antelope, its clouds of birds, belonging to everyone, enjoyed by all."6.

Wovoka's vision spread rapidly throughout the Indian nations. The Ghost Dance was adopted and made suitable to various cultures. Many dancers experienced trances; some dancers were enabled to pierce the boundary between the living and the dead where they encountered relations and close associates known during their earthly life. Some people claimed they received sacred knowledge. Sacred songs developed around the ritual and foretold the restoration of the buffalo.

Government agencies in charge of Indian life on the reservations made every conceivable attempt to suppress not only the Ghost Dance but also all other native traditions, which they feared would make this conquered people less malleable. The customs of the Indians, especially the Ghost Dances caused fear and hysteria among the Christian missionaries; military intervention was sought and resulted in the tragedy of Wounded Knee on the Pine Ridge reservation where the massacre of over two-hundred Lakota men, women and children occurred when the soldiers mowed them down with newly developed Hotchkiss canons on December 29, 1890. To Native Americans, Wounded Knee came to be known as the "United States Holocaust." The Lakota warrior, American Horse, described the massacre. "The women as they were fleeing with their babies were killed together, shot right through, and the women who were heavy with child were also killed. All the Indians fled, and after most of them had been killed, a cry was made that those who were not killed or wounded should come forth and they would be safe. Little boys who were not wounded came out of their places of refuge, and as soon as they came in sight, a number of soldiers surrounded them and butchered them there."7.

One of the most notorious casualties of that day's calamity was the death of Sitting Bull in the nearby reservation of Standing Rock. The fearless warrior was killed along with his adopted brother, Jumping Bull in the wake of the cross-fire between Sitting Bull's armed, loyal coterie and the rifles of the Indian police, sent to apprehend him at the behest of the reservation authorities, who instigated the rumor that Sitting Bull was using the Ghost Dance to incite the Lakota to go on the warpath. The fact remains that Sitting Bull was nowhere near Wounded Knee when he was shot down.

Vivekananda provides his reverence for such a person as Sitting Bull. "The earth is enjoyed by heroes – this is the unfailing truth. Be a hero, always say 'I have no fear'"8.

Next on the chopping block was the Sun Dance, the most sacred ceremony of the Lakota. What really sent the clergy's' teeth on edge was that some of the dancers made offerings of their flesh to the Holy Woman (White Buffalo Calf Maiden) in their gratitude for her benevolence, or at times in the hope of receiving a vision. St. Pierre and Tilda Long Soldier explain, "Among the Lakota, the dancers may further vow to be staked through the skin of their chest or back to the Sun Dance tree (the stakes and cords representing human ignorance), or they may drag a buffalo skull or offer small pieces of flesh from their upper arm. These flesh offerings from the upper arm are generally a sacrifice made by women, although men may make it as well…If a few dancers are fortunate, they may collapse and experience a vision."9.

Vivekananda provides a parallel experience of the compassionate Buddha. "A hawk pounced upon a bird and was about to devour it. In order to save the bird, Buddha gave the hawk his own flesh."10.

The fate of the Indians confined to the reservations was sealed at Wounded Knee; the white authorities relentlessly attempted to suppress the Lakota's free spirit, enjoyed on the open range of the plains, and his communion with all the natural things it provided for his sustenance. From the end of the nineteenth century to the first decades of the twentieth, the Indian appeared on the surface Christianized and Americanized, but on the whole passive and out of sight from the eyes of mainstream America. St. Pierre and Long Soldier lay out the Lakota's predicament – essentially he was a prisoner of war. The authors point out that after incarceration on reservations or worse, the soldier and other dream societies withered like buffalo herds and eventually died out. Priests ministered, and doctors aggressively tried to stamp out the reputation of holy men and women, sending those who wouldn't oblige to prisons and mental hospitals: Lame Deer did some time in county jails; Wallace Black Elk was institutionalized for his "maladjustment ." The government called these people hostile or irreconcilable. Parents who held their children back from schools, or who stood fast in the old traditions, were sent to government run mental asylums – essentially political prisons, according to St. Pierre and Long Soldier.

In Canton South Dakota, these records came to light that those inmates, who never returned home again – and there were many – were buried beneath what is now a public golf course. In the 1990s the Lakota/Dakota people held a ceremony there, to commemorate that terrible spot with a plaque. The authors insinuate that the inmates of these institutions simply died and their relatives were never notified. The authorities simply buried them in a potter's field.

Not all clergy were hardliners of the Father Lindebrner

mold. Father Pierre Jean De Smet was a missionary much respected by the Sioux. He approached the bands on the plains with an open mind and respected their religion and traditions. The Jesuit tried to negotiate a lasting peace between the white people and the Native Americans of the plains; the Indians with great devotion accepted him; the Sioux called him "Black Robe." Father Pierre made the comment that he was more at home at a feast in a tipi than dining with church dignitaries. Father Pierre was said to be even tempered, laughter-loving and without any desire of martyrdom, which frequently interfered with the success of a Jesuit's mission. Sitting Bull referred to the Father and an Indian trader, Major Charles Galpin, "Their tongues are straight. We shall meet him and his friends with arms stretched out, ready to embrace him."11. Father Pierre called Sitting Bull, "generalissimo".

TOLERATION

John Steinbeck made a statement during the 1950s. "The Indians survived our open intention of wiping them out, and since the tide turned they have weathered our good intentions toward them which can be much more deadly." (John Steinbeck, America and Americans).

In time the hardest of the hardliners among the clergy on the reservations passed away, replaced by a younger generation of missionaries with at least a little more open mindedness, but on some issues their resistance was as strong as those who preceded them.

The Native Americans, who remained on the reservations, lived on government handouts, and their poverty was as dire as any in the Third World. But by the 1930s, community standards began to change and racist attitudes moderated somewhat at least toward the red man, many who still lived on reservations at a great distance from the towns and cities of non-Indians. However, Native Americans and non-Indians had had previous encounters. The armed services, to a degree, had integrated many Indians into the mainstream by allowing them participation in its successive wars: the Spanish-American war, and later in both world wars. Many Indians lived in the white world inconspicuously.

The Indian Reorganization Act (1934) was passed in Congress and restored the freedom of tribal religion by abolishing the rules and regulations that prohibited the conduct of tribal religions on reservations. Deloria applauds the significance of this new ruling. "In 1934 under the Indian Reorganization Act, Indian people were finally allowed religious freedom. The missionaries howled in protest, but the ban on Indian religious ceremonies was lifted. Traditional Indians could no longer be placed in prison for practicing old tribal ways. Ceremonies began to be practiced openly, and there were still enough older Indians alive that a great deal of tribal religious traditions were regained."12.

Most of the clergy resisted and butted heads with this milestone of good sense. A Lakota woman rebuked the reactionary attitude and asked an important missionary what his church was doing in "Our" sacred place. "It was sacred long before you came. Those people who died here, whose bodies were thrown on top of one another, they weren't Catholics. They believed in the Great Spirit, the pipe, and the ghost dance. They weren't baptized. And you built a church over them and put a cross here. You made this a place to make money from the tourist who come to see where all those Indians were killed."13.

During this time, the 1930s, the Indian had had his tribal rights restored, but he was still viewed outside the tribal pale as the distant other, succinctly put he was out of sight, out of mind: his picture appeared on highway billboards – a stodgy image portrayed as an old chief, outfitted in eagle-feather headdress, dully smoking his peace pipe; caricatured red men appeared on mail-order homespun remedies for ailing hypochondriacs, a comic stripe Sitting Bull on packaged firecrackers, an Indian face on a 15 cent postage stamp, and an Indian and buffalo emblazoned on an old fashioned nickel.

Leonard Crow Dog rebuffs these misconceptions. "White people depict us in their books and movies as stonyfaced folks with the corners of our mouths turned down, always looking grim. But we are not like that. Among ourselves we joke and laugh. With all that suffering and poverty our people can survive only by laughing at misfortune. That's why we have the sacred clown, heyoka, the hot-cold, forward-backward, upside down contrary. He makes us laugh through our tears. And we have Iktomi, the spider man. He's a trickster, a no-good, but also an inventor, a creator."14.

On Route 66 motorists whiz past a stoic Native American family of vendors: the Navajo weaver has her prized woven blanket for sale; the silversmith displays his handmade sterling silver and turquoise rings. Occasionally a carload of tourists or a family stops to take snapshots of the curious couple in authentic native dress, and then drives away with a few souvenirs from their excursion to the Grand Canyon.

The Indians of America – those ghostly figures that Americans loved and cherished were resurrected by Native American artists and craftspeople, who began to be recognized as their depictions of beautiful landscapes with herds of buffalo and portraits of old tribal chiefs began to appear in art galleries and found their way into the homes of people of means. Remington sculptures of the braided Sioux on horseback or the mounted warrior with his shield, sold out as soon as they hit the shelves of art dealers and antique shops, and were greatly coveted by museums.

Of all the humiliations that Native Americans were subjected to in this token period of open mindedness, were the outrageous stereotypes reinforced on the celluloid of Hollywood's B-westerns: the encircled wagon train is fending off an attack depicted by the parody of the Indian –half naked savages painted in the proverbial red war paint, which is smeared across their faces and bodies (according to Standing Bear, the term "red man" was a name used by white people to denote the custom of painting the skins of children, both male and female with red paint), who are stopped just short of overrunning the defenders – always roughhewn good looking men or ugly ones with a lot of chutzpah or the occasionally lovely young woman, their deadly Winchesters never fail to hit their mark, leaving trails of blood and feathers on the ground. Or on the occasion when the Indian is winning and the wagon train or lonely farmhouse is in danger of being overrun, the movie audience lets out a sigh of relief at the sound of the bugle announcing the arrival of the cavalry. Or when the Indian is not on the warpath, it is a pliant Tonto, the Lone Ranger's Sancho Panza. Standing Bear played in some of these movies, but as an extra. When the Indian was featured in speaking roles, whites played the parts: a Jeff Chandler, an Anthony Quinn, even a Burt Lancaster or the always beautiful Debra Paget. Sitting Bull and Nick Black Elk toured Europe and America with Bill Cody's Wild West Show. Many years later the award winning Dances with Wolves was seen by Native Americans as an honest attempt to redress the egregious sins of Hollywood's past; Indians played the heroic roles of

Indian. Eagle Man of the Rainbow tribe stated, "I hope this is a new beginning for the film industry."

The communal nature of the Indian's personal existence is derived from numerous accounts of the histories of respective tribes. For generations traditional historical literature of Native America was presented as a recital of tribal histories from pre-Columbian culture through the first encounter with whites up to the year 1890 when the Sioux suffered a resounding defeat at Wounded Knee. Deloria explains the change in attitude at the fin-de-siecle. "At that point [1890], the tribe seems to fade gently into history with its famous war chief riding down the canyon into the sunset. Individuals appear within this history only to the extent that they appear to personalize the fortunes of the tribe. A mythical Hiawatha, a sadden Chief Joseph, a scowling Sitting Bull, a sullen Geronimo, all symbolize not living people but the historic fate of a nation overwhelmed by the inevitability of history."15.

ACCEPTANCE

Vivekananda, as we may recall, explains the difference between religious tolerance and acceptance: the former conveys an attitude of a willingness to hear the other's point of view, while all the while, inspite of pantomimed gestures – polite nods and handshakes, interfaith meetings end with the participants complaisantly unconvinced that any other faith can parallel their own. Acceptance, on the other hand, is an eagerness to embrace all religions, as one's own – "So many faiths, so many paths" as Ramakrishna tirelessly repeated. Swamiji said every religion on earth is consciously or unconsciously striving toward this goal.

Tolerance had its own status quo; the Native American

endured the indifference of the non-Indian world with stoic forbearance. Also taken in stride was the public attitude about the Indian, shaped by an opportunistic media, which created the image of a village buffoon, a laughing stock when he was not demonized. History books were nothing more than a cover up for the tragic realities and the theft of Indian lands. The restoration of Native American communal rights and religion made this period easier to swallow than the draconian measures of the missionaries. But even this status quo did not endure, as the perception of non-Indians underwent a radical volte-face as a consequence of the social movements of the 60s of which Lakota radicals both activist and spiritual played a large role. The Indian was not only accepted in the outcome but was ballyhooed. The reader's understanding of this milestone may be clarified by the evolving turn of history, which led to the creation of a positive new image of the Indian.

In the year 2012, the New Age grapevine, using the ancient Mayan calendar as its source, predicted a major shift of global consciousness. When no millenarian event occurred, and no Mayan came forth to substantiate this notion, the pundits were left dazed and tightlipped.

During the nineteen sixties, however, a real shift of global consciousness did occur; the reverberations of this new outlook would impact the world for years to come.

While many things seemed to be in retreat at the time (depending on whose ox was gored), many would agree that an expanded awareness shook up the status quo: the long war in Viet Nam came to an inconclusive halt (no peace treaty was ever signed), and to a degree there were changes in racial and sexist attitudes in terms of tolerance if not acceptance. Even the handicapped community received its share of legislative benefits: wheelchair accessible public buildings, designated parking spaces, and public conveyances designed with the disabled in mind.

People everywhere were leaving their time-honored shackles behind – drawn toward the glasnost of freedom. But this ageless ideal did not occur without a struggle, as thousands of demonstrators put forth outrageous histrionics or creative impromptu pantomime to expand the awareness of an intransigent public. In the United States the Civil Rights movement was at the forefront of protest and belatedly gathered a groundswell of public support, as more people became impressed and sympathetic to Dr. Martin Luther King and his non-violent activism. Other noisy protests followed or coincided with a clamor for equal rights; besides the anti war protest, women, Chicanos and gay people drew public attention to their perception of second class citizenship and demanded that their grievances be redressed by a government whose placating efforts fell on deaf ears. Demonstrations continued and grew more persistent: traffic was tied up in perpetual gridlock in cities and towns; federal buildings were closed and massive sit-ins disrupted the work week; draft boards were harassed as the legitimacy of the draft was called into question: unassailable young people convinced many bemused recruits that the war was not worth dying for. On the whole these raucous rallies were peaceful, but when the police reacted violently to rocks and bottles they claimed were thrown at them, the country became more polarized. But in time support for the war turned unfavorably against it. Other activists with different axes to grind vicariously identified with the limp and passive young people, they watched being hustled into paddy wagons en route to jail. The public was more informed and better educated than ever before.

Less peaceful were resistance movements concurring in

178 BACK TO THE BLANKET

other parts of the world: spontaneous uprisings comprised of students, workers, and peasants carried their struggle to the mountains and countryside or on to university campuses, determined to dislodge corrupt and repressive regimes and foreign colonialism. Tiananmen Squares sprouted up everywhere even before there was a Tiananmen Square in 1989.

In the Olympic Plaza constructed for the 1968 Summer Olympics in Mexico City, the police fired upon throngs of students and other activists when they protested the government's effort to impress arriving foreign dignitaries and athletes with a spruced up national image at the expense of the poor and downtrodden. At the outset of the competition, black athletes of the U.S. Olympic team interrupted the hoopla to stage a silent protest in solidarity with the demonstrators, which caught worldwide attention: heads were bowed, and the stadium was so quiet you could hear a pin drop.

Behind the upsurge of awareness and desire for change was the elusive idea of freedom, which was as out of reach as Tantalus' grapes, but millions continued to struggle for it. Swami Vivekananda believes everything in the universe is struggling for this elusive freedom. "The whole universe is in fact the result of this struggle for freedom. In all combinations every particle is trying to go on its own way, to fly from the other particles; but the others are holding it in check. Our earth is trying to fly away from the sun, and the moon from the earth. Everything has a tendency to infinite dispersion. All that we see in the universe has for its basis this one struggle towards freedom; it is under the impulse of this tendency that the saint prays and the robber robs. When the line of action taken is not a proper one, we call it evil; and when the manifestation of it is proper and high we call it good. But the impulse is the same, the struggle towards freedom. The saint is oppressed with the knowledge of his condition of bondage, and he wants to get rid of it; so he worships God. The thief is oppressed with the idea that he does not possess certain things, and he tries to get rid of that want, to obtain freedom from it; so he steals. Freedom is the one goal of all nature, sentient or insentient; and consciously or unconsciously, everything is struggling towards that goal. The freedom which the saint seeks is very different from that which the robber seeks; the freedom loved by the saint leads him to the enjoyment of infinite, unspeakable bliss, while that on which the robber has set his heart only forges other bonds for his soul."16.

By the early nineteen seventies the public was saturated with the worn out images of unisex armies burning flags and bras as they mocked and jeered uniformed officials. As awareness expanded for receptive minds, it stood in stagnant limbo for minds morally and temperamentally unprepared for it. Thus, a conservative backlash arose to condemn both the government and the "unwashed children of privilege." The conservatives (and they were still in the majority) were too macho to have had any truck with the politicians, who postured with whimpish limp wrists instead of nailed fists when it came time to take the gloves off. The conservatives were anti war, too, because it wasn't being fought decisively enough.

As the images of dissent faded, the public became aware of the American Indian Movement. AIM was the acronym its activists and supporters preferred and it became the catchword in the media. AIM dovetailed with the dissension of the times, but media attention was often on the scrimmage line, but more visible in the local networks wherever Indians were a heavy presence. Comments Leonard Crow Dog, "It was like in the days of the ghost dance. There was a whispering in the air, a faint drumbeat, a hoof beat. It became a roar carried by the four winds: 'a nation is coming, the eagle brought the message.' What was coming called itself AIM, the American Indian Movement."17. Indians from many tribes protested everywhere they held a grievance: sites were selected where treaties had been broken and stillborn promises never kept, on tribal holy grounds, taken away and never returned. Attention was drawn to the substandard conditions on the reservations: the dilapidated housing, the inadequate health care, the lack of suitable water and cultivatable agricultural land. Demonstrations were held in cities where there was disproportional unemployment and discrimination against Native Americans.

Native Americans even fought against the excavation of their burial grounds for archaeological studies and experiments, and ran up against roadblocks, which supported the legal right of looting a few dusty bones and rusty jewelry, as long as they were the remains of Indians not whites. This was in contrast to comparably well off tribes whose reservations rested above the subsoil of rich oil and mineral deposits. The Native Americans demanded a homeland and the return of ceremonial use of lands. During this activism, hundreds of young men and women were arrested but later released from jail by sympathetic judges and juries.

Crow Dog said the fight began in his own backyard. "At the end of 1972 and the beginning of 1973, AIM had come in force to Rapid City to demonstrate, educate, and sensitize the white people there. AIM called South Dakota 'the most racist state in the Union, and Rapid City the most racist town in the state.' In Rapid, Indians were discriminated against in every way. They were made to feel unwelcome in stores, restaurants, and bars. They were called all kinds of names and beaten up. If they got any jobs at all they were paid less than whites."18. During its protest in Rapid City, AIM drew attention to itself by putting up posters: "Welcome To The Most Racist State In The U.S.A. And See South Dakota Last."19.

Leonard Crow Dog comments on AIM's interaction with the shakers and movers of the Civil Rights movement. "Later we went to Harlem [after joining Martin Luther King on a platform] to meet up with some of the Black Power leaders. Lame Deer joked and told Stokely Carmichael, 'Indian kills his enemy, white man skins his friend. What do you do?' Stokely laughed and said, 'We eat them.' This march was a breakthrough. Our tribe got on the map."20.

The American Indians were a natural choice for public attention. They were a colorful and romantic segment of the past, and until they brought their activism into mainstream awareness, they were submerged under the turmoil of better televised causes. Writes Deloria, "When the Indian protest began in the 1960s, white Americans learned that in the remote canyons of the west, the swamplands of the Great Lakes and southeastern United States were seemingly thousands upon thousands of Indians. Perhaps their first response was a sense of outrage and shock. Where were these angry Indians coming from and what was their gripe? They soon discovered that Indians had enjoyed treaty rights for nearly a century. They learned that as resources had been gobbled up by urban America they were in conflict with American Indians over remaining natural resources of the continent, the best which were in Indian hands."21.

Not all resistance was passive and nonviolent, however. Impatience with the slow pace of change, and turning of the judicial cheek in the wake of the murder of Native Americans by whites, sometimes for amusement, sent young militants into a radical tailspin. The coverage on television was spectacular. Angry young militants broke through the restraints and committed overt acts of sabotage, to draw attention to the footdraging nonchalance of the Bureau of Indian Affairs, when it came to equal rights of citizenship for all Indians in the world's oldest democracy. The national headquarters of the BIA was broken in to and thrashed; files from local branches were pilfered and never returned.

During February 1973, a spectacular occupation occurred at Wounded Knee on the Lakota's Pine Ridge reservation of which few could turn a blind eye. The incident was initially sparked by the killing of Wesley Bad Heart Bull, a member of the Lakota by a white patron in a barroom altercation in Buffalo Gap, a small South Dakota town. When a group of Oglala went to the county seat in Custer to protest the lenient sentence imposed on the offender, a small Chamber of Commerce building was set ablaze. Then the Indians, indignant over the insouciance of the local and state police, in pursuit of justice for the victim in Buffalo Gap, occupied the small settlement of Wounded Knee. What could be more symbolic than Wounded Knee? AIM struck at the double standard of American justice. The protesters dramatized the perceived fact that it was not unlawful to kill Indians and compared Buffalo Gap to the Ghost Dance massacre of 1890. At that time not only were the Lakota not accorded justice by an indifferent white government, but the soldiers who shot down scores of women, children and unarmed men actually were rewarded with medals rather than long prison terms.

Leonard Crow Dog points to a survivor of Wounded Knee. "Our close relative and member of our clan, Uncle Dick Fool Bull, was still living, close to ninety years old, and he was a survivor of what happened back in 1890. He was the last flute maker and player in our tribe, and he told me his story many times."22.

During the following two months, Wounded Knee was still in the hands of the occupiers. Law enforcement was sent to remove the activists, which included armed officers of the FBI and local authorities. The tribal police, nick-named the "Goon Squad" surrounded the occupiers and a standoff followed. There were rumors that other AIM activists from different tribes were on the way to join the occupation. As events reached a crescendo – Leonard Crow Dog said that FBI snipers shot and killed three unarmed bystanders, some not even AIM members - public attention became increasingly widespread, as film coverage of the event was televised every night on network news. Sympathetic Hollywood actors made gestures of support: Marlon Brando sent Sasheen Little Feather to reject his winning Oscar for his role in the Godfather, to protest Hollywood's negative stereotyping of Native Americans. Some local churches sided with the demonstrators: asylum was offered to activists, fleeing the bullets of the FBI and vindictive tribal cops; liberal congregations broke through the siege with food and medical supplies earmarked for the dissidents.

The occupation persisted inspite of the Nixon White House's attempt to negotiate a settlement which the Indians said had no teeth. It was only the promise of a delegation sent by the government to discuss its violations of the 1868 Sioux treaty that motivated the occupiers to decamp, but these efforts floundered.

The government moved to incriminate AIM. Two vocal and recognizable leaders (of the Ojibwa nation), who embodied all the grievances and activism of the Indians' protest, were singled out by the Justice Department: Russell Means and Denis Banks. The government put them on trial and planted an undercover agent, Douglas Durham, within the ranks of the protesters and, thus, knew the strategy of the defense. The prosecution's attempt to doctor the evidence and suborn witnesses, who teetered under the cross-examination of a strong defense, resulted in a mistrial declared by the presiding judge. According to Leonard Crow Dog, "The prosecutor put on the stand a witness who swore falsely under oath to have seen Dennis and Russell do certain things at Wounded Knee, when at the time this witness had been a thousand miles away in California. When the judge, Frederick Nichol found out about this, he exploded in anger. For an hour and a half he told the prosecutor and the FBI what he thought of them. He said that all his life he had believed in the FBI and the American system of justice, until this moment...Judge Nichol dismissed all charges, finding the administration of justice had been 'tainted' by 'serious' prosecutorial 'misconduct.' He said, 'I am forced to the conclusion that the prosecutor in this trial had something other than attaining justice foremost in its mind...This case was not prosecuted in good faith or the spirit of justice. The waters of justice have been polluted."23. The fanfare over the siege at Wounded Knee and the acquittal of the defendants pushed the Native American cause to the forefront of public attention.

Then a year later in June 1975, Pine Ridge was in the news again. This time there was violence and the Indians were armed. For some undisclosed reason (Deloria) the FBI had staked out a house just beyond the boundaries of the reservation. The Lakota, apprehensive over the presence of federal agents so close to their sovereign territory, defended themselves, and a shoot out occurred which resulted in the fatalities of two agents. The proof against the Indians was, indeed, very sketchy, according to Peter Matthiessen. In his book, In the Spirit of Crazy Horse: the bodies revealed multiple wounds, but the botched evidence failed to convince many impartial people who followed the headlines. Speculation was widespread that the Justice Department planted the evidence and conspired with the FBI to make it stick. But on the other hand, witnesses testified that the Indians had fired brief, sporadic shots in self-defense and summarily fled the scene. Several members of AIM were convicted. Leonard Peltier was singled out. Matthiessen outlines the many discrepancies and flagrant illegalities conducted by the prosecuting attorneys to secure Peltier's conviction, and he was imprisoned in a federal penitentiary with a long sentence.

During the same year, the momentum of political activism began to subside: the Viet Nam war drew to a close, and the resistance movements vacated sites that over the years became synonymous with the struggle, and left the streets of the cities to bobbing Hari Krishnas. Some anti-war remnants coalesced with other causes whose rank and file remained unreconciled to the government's carrot and stick approach. Less cathartic than the participatory democracy of student brigades and campus teach-ins were the less than revolutionary tactics organized around distributing leaflets, filling town hall meetings with audiences willing to listen, and the endless tedious discussion groups to decide on more discussion groups. A new consensus was organized around the assumption of working within the system to overthrow it. AIM, too, would have to have its day in court.

Still fresh in the public eye were the Lakota uprisings on and around Pine Ridge, and a growing empathy stirred in the minds of non-Indians around the whole gamut of a people whose identity had been locked within a realm of mystery and shadow.

Carter Camp, a militant AIM member pegged the attention

Pine Ridge and other AIM hotspots received in the media. "As long as we are good Boy Scouts behaving ourselves, nobody gives a shit. But as soon as we're waving guns, the media come running. If it takes waving guns to get our grievances before the public, than that's what we have to do."24. Wounded Knee received the attention of the media all over the world. All of AIM's leaders "had a good mouth." They were powerful speakers who could draw wonderful word pictures. But South Dakota Senator George McGovern, iconic liberal champion of the rights of racial minorities and the downtrodden had little room in his heart for AIM. When he put in a cameo appearance at Wounded Knee, Leonard Crow Dog noted, "He said he had not much time for us, he had to get back to Rapid [City] to change into a clean shirt. Russell [Means] said, 'He's worried about his shirt. We're worried about seeing another sun rise."25.

As mainstream support for the Indian cause picked up, serious writers, many of them Native American, put forth a concerted effort to overcome the fallacious notions of past non-Indian kitsch; indiscreet publishers flooded the market with half baked pot boilers of New Age theorists, and many Native Americans took issue with the ballyhoo. Books were written to dramatize the tragedy of the Ghost Dance, and the federal government's ignominious confiscation of Indian lands. Dee Brown's Bury My Heart At Wounded Knee dovetailed with the times and informed an ingenuous public about the issues glossed over in discarded history books, sometimes designed to obfuscate the Indian point of view. Biographies of Nick Black Elk and Luther Standing Bear were reprinted and enjoyed widespread circulation. When the dust of the nineteen seventies settled, the non-Indian community had come full circle. The Native American was accepted and acceptance sometimes arrived with a bear hug.

At one time the Indian was pilloried for his "pagan" beliefs, a century later his postmodern aficionados placed him on a pedestal.

Leonard Crow Dog had taken the rap for the militancy at Pine Ridge and elsewhere; he was incarcerated, moved from one federal prison to another. Leonard galvanized this new spirit and attitude toward Native America; even the prison population at Leavenworth spontaneously offered its approval. "When they released me into the general prison population, the inmates already knew about me. They struck their clenched fists through the bars and shouted, 'Crow Dog! Crow Dog! Crow Dog! In this way they welcomed me. They took one another by the hands through the bars, some whites, some Indians, some blacks. They chanted a prayer for me, a prayer for a Lakota medicine man."26. Crow Dog was eventually released, and the charges against him were dropped, as a mistrial was declared.

Father Steltenkamp took the pulse of this new attitude. "[That these extremes] historically have created either a genocidal posture toward Indians, or a mentality almost deifying their imagined attributes. The former has bred racism, while the latter has incarnated the bubblings of Ponce De Leon's mythical fountain of youth. Somewhere between these extremes lies the reality of flesh-and-blood Native America."27.

To young people and many of those of an older generation, the Indian was suddenly "cool". Students from prestigious universities joined the avalanche of visitors making field trips to Indian reservations. Activists of every stripe flooded Pine Ridge and Rosebud: Journalists, intellectuals, anthropologists, social workers, nuns and priests arrived like Peace Corps volunteers. Some people came to sit at the feet and learn sacred knowledge from bonafide medicine men, others to offer feel-good generosity, or to make new beneficiaries of their savior faire.

One example of this new spirit of bonhomie was the bad result of good intentions – the sensationalism of some New Age writers and journalists to remake the Native American in a hip, new image, which misrepresented the culture and ceremony they intended to explain. Lakota spokesperson, Mitchell Zephier explains the damage done by New Age good intentions. "If you think about the Sun Dance or the Buffalo Calf ceremony, they were all performed for the good of the people. You might have only one young lady going through the ceremony, but all the people witness that, and they absorb the transmission of values from the elderly people.

"What it reminds me of is that there is a right way to live, a right way to do things. A lot of these New Age people, because they are so spiritually hungry, are like people starved for food – they grab anything and eat it without question. Today there is a lot of controversy about whether to let New Age people participate in ceremonies, but like the lies in these books it's sad, because for many years now the dominant society has tried to eradicate native beliefs. Now people think they can make them up, create history and culture, and play with our beliefs." 28.

Not all non-Indians came to Pine Ridge on a lark or for the purpose of vicarious atonement. Many people arrived with a willingness to learn and to accept new values which hitherto could only be gotten from books. The cresting of the Indian movement 1972-1990, was the adoption of some Native American beliefs and practices by large segments of non-Indian society, who were truly interested and were not following a trendy fad. The medicine-wheel was a feature most readily adopted by white people. The pipe and the seven directions to which Plains Indians pray, oriented eager non-Indians to the natural world, as were symbolic costumes that they believed would bring them closer to nature.

A significant result of the deluge of attention and goodwill directed toward the American Indian was a new sense of identity accompanied by a tremendous surge of interest in traditional religion and customs among native peoples. Standing Bear referred to this phenomenon as "going back to the blanket." Deloria observes, "In isolated places on reservations, a gathering of people is taking place and much of the substance of the old way of life is starting to emerge. Some keen observers predict that within a decade [1990s] people serving on tribal councils will have to have a full traditional ceremonial life to get elected."29.

Again Deloria, "On the reservations we are seeing amazing resiliency in restoring the old ceremonies. A massive shift in allegiance is occurring in most tribes away from Christianity and secularism and back toward traditional ways. A surprising high percentage of Native American clergy are also doing traditional ceremonies and urban area churches are often the scenes of traditional healing ceremonies. The Native American clergy are to be congratulated for their efforts to bring the two religious traditions together, but it is clear that no synthesis will take place. In almost every instance the effect of merging the two traditions is to bring attention to traditional ways to the detriment of the particular Christian denomination. The result is the semblance of a national Indian religion is being born that incorporates major Indian themes. As people are sensitized to this new religious milieu being dissatisfied with lack of specificity in this religious activity, they return to more precise practices of their own tribes. Thus, it appears that traditional religions in some form will transcend the inroads that contemporary American culture has made."30.

Standing Bear Paxton, a Lakota spiritual leader states the meaning of the paradox. "When I am asked about my religion, I talk about being Episcopalian, but for my spirituality, I go with my Indian ways."31. Even Nick Black Elk became a Catholic Catechist among his people.

One humorous, off-color paradox to the return of the blanket was observed by Deloria when some Christian clergy seriously sought the protective shelter of the same blanket. "The rise of New Age spiritualism has most definitely intruded into the behavior patterns of contemporary Christianity. Hardly a day goes by that my work is not interrupted by a renegade Protestant minister who wants me to send him to an Indian medicine man for spiritual counseling or by the news that some Christian church is now vesting its bishops and pastors in buckskins and feathers or purchasing crystals for its rituals. Groups of American Indians have now made presentations at most of the Christian church national meetings and given their version of the reverence for nature. And a considerable number of Christian clergy have tried to do some version of the sweat lodge or vision quest."32.

Deloria concludes, "All of these things, taken together, make it seem as if we are now approaching a time when a new kind of religion will make itself manifest to us. If we view all of this struggling for meaning in a world in which institutions and beliefs are rapidly eroding, then it seems likely that people are merely sorting out the correlation between beliefs and experiences."33.

Vivekananda would agree with such an observation. The Swami told a group of American disciples at Thousand Island Park on Long Island that, "the age of St. Paul, however, is gone. We are to be the new lights for this age. A self adjusting organization is the great need of our time. When we can get one that will be the last religion of the world. The wheel of the world must revolve, and we should help it, not hinder."34.

What the Swami had in mind was the advent of Ramakrishna's presence and teachings he believed would be the spark to an age of acceptance. "From the very date that he [Ramakrishna] was born, has sprung the Satya-yuga (Golden Age). Henceforth there is an end to all sorts of distinctions and everyone down to the Chandala [untouchables] will be a sharer in the Divine Love. The distinction between man and woman, between the rich and the poor, the literate and illiterate, Brahman and Chandalas – he lived to root out all. And he was the harbinger of peace – the separation between Hindus and Mohammedans, between Hindus and Christians, all are now things of the past. That fight about distinction that there was, belonged to another era. In this Satya-yuga the tidal wave of Shri Ramakrishna's Love has unified all."35.

Notes

Preface

1.   Swami Vivekananda, The Complete Works of Swami Vivekananda, 'Calcutta, (1989 ed.), 203.

2.   Christopher Isherwood, Ramakrishna and His Disciples, Simon & Schuster, N.Y., 1965,1

3.   Pravrajika Vrajaprana, Vedanta A Simple Introduction, Vedanta Press, Hollywood, 1999, 63-64

4.   Swami Vivekananda, The Complete Works of Swami Vivekananda, Advaita Ashram, Calcutta, (2001, ed.) V. 4, 168

5.   ibid

6.   ibid, 169

7.   Sister Nivedita, Kali, The Mother, Advaita Ashrama, Calcutta, 75-76,

8.   C.W., V.4, 171 (2001 ed.)

9.   Ajit Mookejee, Kali, The Feminine Force, Destiny Books, Rochester, V.T.,1988

10.   C.W., V.7, 4 (2001 ed.)

11.   Vrajaprana, 67

12.   ibid, 54
13.   Isherwood, 23
14.   Swami Nikhilananda, The Gospel of Ramakrishna, (abridged ed.) Ramakrishna-Vivekananda Center, N.Y., 1958, 96-97
15.   C.W., V.5, 392, (2001 ed,)
16.   G.R., (abridged ed), 435
17.   ibid, 404
18.   ibid, 114
19.   C.W., V.1, 4 (2001 ed.)
20.   ibid, 3-4
21.   ibid, 19
22.   Sister Nivedita, 71
23.   Swami Nikhilananda, Holy Mother, Ramakrishna-Vivekananda Center, N.Y., 1962, 134
24.   Richard Epstein, The Mother of Songs, Temple Universal Publishing, Hollywood, 2007, 65
25.   ibid, 53
26.   Swami Saradananda, The Great Master, Sri Ramakrishna Math, Mylapore, 1952, 290
27.   The Gospel of the Holy Mother, Sri Ramakrishna Math, Madras, 1984, 75

Introduction
1.   W.Y. Evans-Wentz, Cuchama and Sacred Mountains, Swallow Press, Chicago, 1981, 159
2.   Swami Saradananda, Sri Ramakrishna and His Divine Play, (edited by Swami Chetanananda, Vedanta Society of St. Louis, 2003), 154
3.   John (Fire) Lame Deer & Richard Erdoes, Lame Deer, Seeker of Visions, Washington Square Press, Pocket Books, N.Y., 1970, 96-97
4.   ibid, 146
5.   Charles Alexander Eastman (Ohiyesa), The Soul of the Indian, Dover Publications, Inc., Mineola, N.Y., 2003, 9
6.   Luther Standing Bear, Land of the Spotted Eagle, University of Nebraska Press, Lincoln, 2006, 123

7.   Mark St. Pierre & Tilda Long Soldier, Walking in the Sacred Manner, Simon & Schuster, N.Y., 1995, 211-212
8.   Vine Deloria Jr. God is Red, Fulcrum Publishing, Golden Co., 1994,45

Chapter 1
1.   Standing Bear, 45
2.   L.D., 226

Chapter 2
1.   Standing Bear, 226
2.   Deloria, op cit Standing Bear, 91
3.   Vivekananda, Letters of Swami Vivekananda, Advaita Ashrama, Calcutta, 1998, 300-301
4.   L.D., 113
5.   Richard Epstein, The Mirror With Two Faces, op cit Prescott, 2011
6.   The Gospel of the Holy Mother, Sri Sarada Devi, (Anthology) Sri Ramakrishna Math, Madras, 29
7.   C.W., V.1, 209, (2001 ed.)

Chapter 3

1.   Richard Epstein, Walking in Beauty, A Morning Star Publication in collaboration with Dry Bones Press, Inc., Roseville, Ca., 2001, 78
2.   ibid, 79
3.   ibid

Chapter 4
1.   C.W., V.1, 374-375, (2001 ed.)
2.   Swami Vivekananda, The Yogas and Other Works, Ramakrishna –Vivekananda Center, N.Y. 1953, 716
3.   C.W., V.2, 429, (1946 ed.)
4.   W.I.B., 83
5.   Evans –Wentz, op cit, Ohiyesa, 114

Chapter 5

1. C.W., V.2, 425 (1946 ed.)
2. ibid
3. W.I.B., 51
4. R.D.P., 121
5. W.I.B., 56
6. Swami Vivekananda, Inspired Talks, Ramakrishna-Vivekananda Center, N.Y., 1958, 25

Chapter 6
1. W.I.B. 102
2. The Yogas, 901

Chapter 7
1. C.W., V.2, 91 (1946 ed.)
2. W.I.B., 107
3. ibid, 107

Chapter 8
1. Arlene Hirschfeldar & Paulette Molin, The Encyclopedia of Native American Religions, Facts on File, N.Y., 1992, 49
2. John Neihardt, Black Elk Speaks, University of Nebraska Press, Lincoln, 188
3. L.D., 119
4. ibid
5. R.D.P., 232

Chapter 9

1. C.W., V.2, 223-224 (2001 ed.)
2. Swami Nikhilananda, The Gospel of Ramakrishna, Ramakrishna-Vivekananda Center, N.Y., 2007, 533
3. Ohiyesa, 44
4. L.D., 135-136
5. W.S.M., 121-122

6.   Evans -Wentz, 124
7.   W.I.B., 118

Chapter 10
1.   L.D., 100
2.   W.I.B., 58
3.   C.W., V.2, 206 (1946 ed.)
4.   L.D., 103
5.   W.I.B., 59
6.   Octavio Paz, New York Review of Books, December
6, 1990

Chapter 11
1.   Letters, 246
2.   Royal Hassick, The Sioux, University of Oklahoma
Press, Norman, 1964, 338
3.   Ohiyesa, 41
4.   W.S.M., 99
5.   ibid, 100
6.   ibid, 101
7.   ibid, 102
8.   ibid
9.   ibid, 199
10.   C.W., V.1, 421 (2001 ed.)
11.   Swami Nikhilananda (translator), Sri Sarada Devi,
The Holy Mother, Her teachings and Conversations, Skylight
Paths, Publishing, Woodstock, V.T. 2004, 9
12.   ibid, 155
13.   C.W., V.7, 58 (2001 ed.)
14.   Teachings and Conversations, 141-142
15.   C.W., V.1, 403 (2001 ed.)
16.   C.W., V.5, 266 (2001 ed.)

Chapter 12
1.   L.D. 29
2.   G.R., 108 (2007 ed.)
3.   Wallace Black Elk & William Lyon, Black Elk, The

Sacred Ways of a Lakota, Harper, San Francisco, 1991, 37
4.   G.R. 135 (2007 ed.)
5.   W.I.B., 30

Chapter 13
1.   Mary Winters & Nancy Wood, (anthology), Many
Winters, Doubleday, N.Y.,1974
2.   Hassrick, 263
3.   G.R., 135 (2007 ed.)
4.   Letters, 426
5.   L.D., 240
6.   ibid
7.   ibid
8.   ibid, 241
9.   Sheila Moon, Changing Woman and Her Sisters,
Guild for Psychological Studies, Publishing House, op cit
Black Elk, Black Elk Speaks, 4
10.   L.D., 241
11.   Hassrick, 263
12.   L.D., 242
13.   ibid, 248n
14.   ibid, 242
15.   Leonard Crow Dog, Crow Dog, Harper Perennial,
N.Y., 1996, 150
16.   L.D., 244
17.   ibid, 245
18.   Standing Bear, 202
19.   ibid
20.   L.C.D., 155
21.   Black Elk Speaks, 96-97
22.   C.W., V.7, 26-27 (2001 ed.)

Chapter 14
1.   Swami Brahmavidyananda, Seeing Beyond the Circle,
op cit Vivekananda, 107-108, Temple Universal Publishing,
Hollywood, 2005
2.   Epstein, Mother of Songs, 129-130, Temple Universal
Publishing, Hollywood, 2005

3.   Standing Bear. 203-204
4.   ibid, 209
5.   C.W., V.4, 47, (2001 ed.)
6.   Ohiyesa, 33
7.   L.C.D. 153
8.   C.W., V. 1, 422, (2001 ed.)
9.   Ohiyesa, 34
10.   Standing Bear, 193
11.   Swami Vivekananda, Talks with Swami Vivekananda, Advaita Ashrama, Calcutta, 1985, 153
12.   W.B.E, 122
13.   LC.D., 20
14.   ibid,   22
15.   C.W.,V.2, 310-311 (2001 ed.)
16.   ibid, 311-312
17.   C.W., V.1.,400 (2001 ed.)

Chapter 15
1.   Joseph Epes Brown, The Sacred Pipe, University of Oklahoma, Norman, 1953, 37
2.   R.D.P., 193
3.   W.S.M., 46
4.   W.B.E., 36
5.   C.W., V.1, 98-99 (2001 ed.)
6.   C.W., V.2, 319 (1946 ed.)
7.   Evans-Wentz, 144
8.   Standing Bear, 46-47
9.   Sri Sarada Devi, The Holy Mother, 239
10.   W.B.E., 73
11.   Standing Bear, 208
12.   L.D., 100
13.   ibid, 174
14.   R.D.P., 635
15.   C.W., V.3, 52 (2001 ed.)

Chapter 16
1.   C.W., V.1, 147-148 (2001 ed.)

2.   William Powers, Sacred language, University of Oklahoma Press, Norman, 1986,30
3.   W.B.E., 55
4.   W.S.M., 36
5.   Black Elk Speaks, 85-86
6.   C.W., V.1, 157-159 (2001 ed.)

Chapter 17
1.   W.I.B., 124
2.   ibid
3.   Bureau of American Ethnology, Smithsonian Institute, wash. D.C.,1907, 62-63
4.   C.W., V.7, 25-26 (2001 ed.)
5.   W.I.B, 127
6.   L.C.D., 159
7.   W.I.B., 128
8.   Deloria, 251-252
9.   W.I.B., 128
10.   The Yogas, 808-809

Chapter 18
1.   W.S.M., St. Pierre & Tilda Long Soldier, op cit Peter Furst, Stones, Bones, and Skins, 24
2.   Stanley Vestal, Sitting Bull, Champion of the Sioux, University of Oklahoma Press, Norman, 1965, 150-151
3.   ibid
4.   Black Elk Speaks, 129
5.   Vestal, 175
6.   Standing Bear, 203
7.   Black Elk Speaks, 203
8.   W.S.M., 106
9.   ibid, 25-26
10.   Black Elk Speaks, 199
11.   ibid, 201
12.   ibid
13.   ibid, 203
14.   ibid, 204-205

15.   The Yogas, 596
16.   W.B.E., 35
17.   ibid, 176
18.   ibid
19.   ibid, 178
20.   Sacred Language, 155-156
21.   Deloria, 250
22.   Letters, 316
23.   W.S.M., 51-52
24.   ibid, 53
25.   Teachings and Conversations, 233
26.   ibid, 172-173
27.   ibid, 158
28.   W.B.E., 54
29.   W.S.M., 127
30.   W.B.E., 26
31.   Talks, 461

Chapter 19
1.   W.I.B., 136
2.   ibid, 137
3.   ibid
4.   L.D., 53-54
5.   ibid, 34-35
6.   Black Elk Speaks, 27
7.   ibid, 26
8.   ibid, 41
9.   ibid, 37
10.   ibid
11.   ibid, 47
12.   G.R., 833-834 (2007 ed.)
13.   Black Elk Speaks 49
14.   L.D., 61
15.   C.W., V.2, 355-356 (2001 ed.)

Chapter 20
1.   W.B.E., 70

2.   ibid
3.   Michael Steltenkamp, The Sacred Vision, The Paulist Press, Ramsey, N.J., 1982, 39
4.   L.D., 167
5.   Steltenkamp, 43
6.   L.C.D., 85
7.   L.D., 170
8.   Ed McGaa, (Eagle Man), Rainbow Tribe, Harper, San Francisco, 1994, 109
9.   L.D., 170-171
10.   William Powers, Yuwipi, University of Nebraska Press, Lincoln, 1982, 10
11.   C.W., V.1, 373 (2001 ed.),
12.   Yuwipi, 92
13.   ibid, 9
14.   Hassrick, 274
15.   Rainbow Tribe, 10
16.   C.W., V.1, 264 (2001 ed.)
17.   Hassrick, 275
18.   Yuwipi, 94
19.   Talks, 66-67
20.   ibid
21.   Yuwipi, 93-94
22.   Hirschfeldar, & Molin, 47

Chapter 21
1.   Ohiyesa, 21
2.   Deloria, 201
3.   L.D., 34-35
4.   W.S.M., 10
5.   Standing Bear, 170
6.   Ohiyesa, 28
7.   L.D., 63-64
8.   Sacred Language, 189
9.   Hassrick, 135
10.   L.D., 106
11.   The Yogas, 706-707

Chapter 22
1.   W.I.B. 76
2.   W.S.M., 167
3.   Inspired Talks, 50-51
4.   Standing Bear, 212
5.   L.D., 27
6.   ibid, 112-113
7.   Nancy Bonvillain, Native American Religion, Chelsea
House Publishers, N.Y., 1996, 88
8.   Talks, 161
9.   W.S.M., 18,
10.   G.R., 948 (2007 ed.)
11.   Vestal, 99
12.   Deloria, 240
13.   L.C.D., 192
14.   ibid, 60
15.   Deloria, 27
16.   C.W., V.1, 108-109 (2001 ed.)
17.   L.C.D., 159
18.   ibid, 180
19.   ibid
20.   ibid, 170
21.   Deloria, 4
22.   L.C.D., 185
23.   ibid, 222
24.   ibid, 200
25.   ibid
26.   ibid, 235
27.   Steltenkamp, 4
28.   W.S.M., 206
29.   Deloria, 43
30.   ibid, 253
31.   W.S.M., 20
32.   Deloria, 234-235
33.   ibid
34.   Inspired Talks, 45
35.   Letters, 207

BIBLIOGRAPHY

1.   Black Elk, Wallace & Lyon William, The Sacred Ways of a Lakota, Harper, San Francisco, 1991
2.   Bonvillain, Nancy, Native American Religion, Chelsea House Publishers, N.Y., 1996
3.   Crow Dog, Leonard & Erdoes, Richard, Crow Dog, Harper Perennial, N.Y., 1995
4.   Deloria, Vine, God is Red, Fulcrum Publishing, Golden, Co., 1994
5.   Eastman, Charles (Ohiyesa), The Soul of the Indian, Dover Publications, Inc., Minelola, N.Y., 2003
6.   Epstein, Richard F., Walking in Beauty, a Morning Star Publication in collaboration with Dry Bones Press, Inc., Roseville, Ca, 2001
7.   Epstein, Richard F., The Mother of Songs, Temple Universal Publishing, Hollywood, 2007
8.   Hassrick, Royal, The Sioux, University of Oklahoma, Norman, 1964
9.   Hirschfeldar & Molin Paulette, The Encyclopedia of Native American Religions, Facts On File, N.Y., 1992
10.   Lame Deer & Erdoes, Richard, Lame Deer Seeker of Visions, Washington Square Press, N.Y., 1972i
11.   Neihardt, John, Black Elk Speaks, University of Nebraska Press, Lincoln, 1988
12.   Swami Nikhilananda, Sri Sarada Devi, The Holy Mother, Her Teachings and Conversations, Skylight Paths Publishing, Woodstock, V.T., 2004
13.   Swami Nikhilananda, The Gospel of Sri Ramakrishna, Ramakrishna-Vivekananda Center, N.Y., 2007
14.   Powers, William, Sacred Language, The Nature of Supernatural Discourse in Lakota, University of Oklahoma Press, Norman, 1986
15.   Powers, William, Yuwipi, University of Nebraska

Press, Lincoln, 1982

16.   St. Pierre, Mark, & Long Soldier, Tilda, Walking in the Sacred Manner, Simon & Schuster, N.Y., 1995

17.   Swami Saradananda, (Swami Chetananda, editor), Sri Ramakrishna and His Divine Play, Vedanta Society of St. Louis, 2003

18.   Standing Bear, Luther, Land of the Spotted Eagle, University of Nebraska, Lincoln, 2006

19.   Steltenkamp, Michael, The Sacred Vision, Paulist Press, N.Y., 1982

20.   Vestal, Stanley, Sitting Bull, Champion of the Sioux, University of Oklahoma, Norman, 1965

21.   Swami Vivekananda, The Complete Works of Swami Vivekananda, Advaita Ashrama, Kolkata, 2001

22.   Swami Vivekananda, Inspired Talks, Ramakrishna-Vivekananda Center, N.Y., 1987

23.   Swami Vivekananda, Talks with Swami Vivekananda, Advaita Ashrama, Calcutta, 1985

24.   Swami Vivekananda, The Yogas and Other Works, Ramakrishna-Vivekananda Center, N.Y., 1953

Also by this author
Fiction
> The Children of Aquarius
> Ali: A Girl of The Sacramento Streets
> W.W.W.DropDead.Com

Historical
> Old Mok: The Story of a Gold Camp
> Columbia: The Town That Midas Touched

Spiritual
> Walking in Beauty: Native American Vedanta

The Mother of Songs: The Universal Mother
The Sandalwood Tree: The Mystic Path, East and
West
The Mirror With Two Faces: Quetzalcoatl, The
Toltec Mystic
My Brothers Keeper, Padre Pio: From a Man to a God

Printed in Great Britain
by Amazon